FOR THE PEOPLE

TIME TO TAKE OUR COUNTRY BACK!

I.VICENTE

VC

V

PUBLISHING

ALSO BY I.VICENTE

The Courage to Be Different (Second Edition)

Divergent Lives

This book is for all the people who proudly call the United States of America home, and whose belief in freedom, prosperity, and individual liberty is unwavering.

Table of Contents

Prologue

I decided to write this book to give an American citizen's voice to the people's general dissatisfaction with how our leaders in Washington have managed or, more accurately, mismanaged the people's affairs. The constant bickering between Congress and the Executive branch of our government has resulted in years of stagnation. It is a lack of progress that makes most Americans feel as though we are sliding backward rather than moving forward. That has caused far too many Americans to lament the demise of the American dream of prosperity and upward mobility. We crave the creation of a seemingly elusive positive environment for our children and future generations.

America is still the greatest country in the world, but it is maligned with many challenges that have been ignored or exacerbated by our leaders. The American people are fed up, tired, and angry. It is time for the people to rise up and take our country back.

It is time that every American remembers the influential words spoken by the 16th President of the United States, Abraham Lincoln, when in delivering the Gettysburg address on November 19, 1863, he said, in conclusion:

"... that this nation, under God, shall have a new birth of freedom—and that government of the people, by the people, for the people, shall not perish from the earth."[1]

Today we are constantly bombarded with useless rhetoric on critical subjects from the economy; to immigration; jobs and unemployment; health care; income inequality; national security; geo-political tragedies and challenges; and email server "mistakes." Yet, it feels as if all this noise spewed at the American people by our politicians and the news media is nothing more than a smokescreen to make us dizzy enough that we fail to see what is really being done with our country's affairs.

The national debt of the United States of America was $10 trillion in 2008. Today, 2015, it is $18.5 trillion—and rising. To put this important fact into perspective, the country accumulated its first trillion dollars of debt in 1981, fully 205 years after the birth of our nation. Yet, it took only 403 days to accumulate our most recent trillion, according to the site Informationstation.org. I will get into this debt and its long-term implications later in the book, but suffice it to say that it is highly hypocritical for the President of the United States to chastise us as individuals for living above our means, yet he drives our country into the ground and buries us for generations in mountains of debt. President Obama has added more than $1 trillion to the country's debt just in the last year. Obama has added $6 trillion to the debt since he took office seven years ago, the largest increase to date under any U.S. president. By comparison, during the eight-year presidency of George W. Bush, the debt soared by $4.9 trillion.[2] And we still have one more year of Obama's presidency.

As Americans and voters we must be skeptical and highly analytical of everything that the politicians and even the news media tell us. They are all masters of oratory and know how to push our buttons. Let's not be fooled any longer!

I remember the speech that President Obama gave in February 2010, when we were in the midst of the great recession. People were hurting everywhere in the country. Jobs were being lost; people were having their homes foreclosed on in record numbers, regardless of income level; even illegal immigrants were returning to their countries of origin as the prospects for day laborers dried up here, and housing construction collapsed. Obama told Americans during a speech in New Hampshire: "When times are tough, you tighten your belts. You don't go buying a boat when you can barely pay your mortgage. You don't blow a bunch of cash on Vegas when you're trying to save for college. You prioritize. You make tough choices."

Was he willing to lead Americans by setting an example consistent with his reprimand? Here is where what I call the audacity of hypocrisy becomes apparent: That very same month, over the President's Day weekend, while the country was "tightening its belt," collectively and as individuals, Michelle Obama, according to Judicial Watch, the public interest group that investigates and fights government corruption, went on a ski vacation with her two daughters at a cost to taxpayers of at least $81,182.99.

In August of that same year, again while in the midst of the recession, Michelle Obama went on another vacation to Spain at a cost to taxpayers of $467,585.00.

Leaders lead by example, and President Obama has shown repeatedly that what applies to the American people does not apply to him and the First Family. It is understandable that Americans who were suffering to find this outrageous and incredibly insensitive. How else can this be explained, other than as an audacious display of hypocrisy? The president's supporters might say that previous presidents have done the same or worse. Perhaps, but we all must remember that one of Barack Obama's campaign promises was to change the way Washington works.

Barack Obama's campaign slogan in the 2008 presidential race was "Change we can believe in." Some things have certainly changed over the past seven years, but not in a positive way for Americans and the country.

That does not mean that the First Family cannot go on vacations, but spending half a million dollars of the people's money on a single vacation during difficult economic times is wrong and shows a lack of genuine concern for the people. I suppose that Michelle Obama found many reasons to be proud of her country once

Barack Obama became president. She and the Obama family have enjoyed lavish vacations paid for by beleaguered taxpayers, many of whom are unable to take their families on a single annual vacation.

We are frequently reminded of her statement at a speech in Milwaukee in 2008, when then-Senator Barack Obama was campaigning for the presidency, and Mrs. Obama remarked that "For the first time in my adult lifetime, I am really proud of my country, and not just because Barack has done well, but because I think people are hungry for change."

While she may have been appealing to the sentiments of those Americans in search of government change that would improve their lives, Michelle Obama's statement should have been viewed as a dangerous and unpatriotic motive behind the Obamas' drive to the White House. This is an Ivy League-educated lawyer, a successful woman who insults Americans by suggesting that Americans were only now "hungry for change" and she had not had any reason to be proud to be an American until her husband was enjoying success on the campaign trail.

It is inconceivable that she was never before as an adult proud of America. Her attitude in making that statement suggested that the success they had enjoyed as adults could have happened in any other country and so there was nothing special about America. Perhaps they could have had that same success and more in Russia, Iran, Pakistan, Kenya, or Indonesia!

"The American people can ill afford to keep sending the First Family on vacations around the globe," stated Judicial Watch President Tom Fitton. "There needs to be greater sensitivity to the costs borne by taxpayers for these personal trips. It is hypocritical for President Obama to fire GSA officials for wasteful conference spending, while his family went on a luxury vacation in the Costa del Sol Spain that cost taxpayers nearly half a million dollars."

America, this is our country! We must remember that our politicians work for the people, the citizens of the United States of America. Remember that the Constitution preamble starts with "We the people." It seems that once a politician gets into office, more often than not he or she acts as if they can do whatever they want regardless of the wishes of the people. Often their actions and decisions are presented to us as being the will of "the people." Each time I hear the President of the United States speak of his intention to sign a piece of legislation, whether a bill that passed through Congress, or more appropriately these days an Executive Action, he goes before the media and declares that "this is what the American people want." That, however, is an illusion used to declare a political legitimacy, creating a sense of unanimity that is misleading and abusive.

When President Obama uses that phrase, does he refer to the people who voted for him, or 100 percent of the citizens of the country, or 100 percent of the U.S. population? Each of these carries a very different representation. Of the people who voted in the 2012 presidential election, 51.1 percent or 65,915,796 voted for Obama, and 47.2 percent or 60,933,500 voted for Mitt Romney. Although Obama won both the Electoral College and the popular vote, he did not have the support of all the people. Regardless of the metric used to make the conscious assertion that he is doing "what the American people want," it is nothing more than an illusion used to stamp the people's approval on legislation or proposed legislation that perhaps a fraction of us want or will benefit from. It is a dangerous abuse of power that most of us do not give much time to analyze as we go about our daily lives. We hear it and accept it, even if we do not agree with it.

The president, senators, and representatives in the House, for the most part, count on people forgetting the details of their discontent and focusing more on their day-to-day lives. Certainly, we are all too busy these days looking for jobs or remaining employed; taking care of our children; cooking and cleaning; and staying on top of our bills to worry too much about the decisions being made in Washington. The cynicism with which we view Washington politics has only gotten worse under Barack Obama.

I had a conversation recently with a lawyer acquaintance who told me that while he is dissatisfied with much of the information he gathers from the news media about events in the government and disagrees with Obama, he doesn't do anything about it because he is too busy running his day-to-day life and business. While that is understandable, I believe it is precisely what our leaders know will happen. That is what they count on happening.

But we have to actively and vigorously question the actions of our government leaders and hold them accountable to us, the people.

The purpose of this book is to provide a template of information and insight that will help people determine who are our best candidates to return our government to the people. We must return our country to the level of domestic and international leadership and prosperity that America has been known for throughout its history. We must ensure our safety. We must make sure that there are opportunities for economic growth for all Americans. According to the voting statistics at the Statistic Brain Research Institute, there are approximately 218,959,000 Americans eligible to vote, and of those approximately 146,311,000 registered to vote. Obviously, the numbers fluctuate as the population in the country changes. In the 2012 presidential election 126,144,000 Americans voted. That is only 57.5 percent of total eligible voters who exercised their right at the ballot box in 2012. What will motivate more Americans to vote?

My hope is that by wading through the massive clutter of rhetoric cunningly dished out by candidates, we will be able to concentrate on the essential skills and dedication to America's values of each of them to make the best decision in electing a new president in 2016. It is with a sense of urgency that we must elect the best candidate who will restore America to greatness.

We cannot afford to elect another President of the United States by ignoring red flags ever again. Americans, including most of the media, ignored Obama's ideological views for America; his association with Jeremiah Wright and Bill Ayers; and Michelle Obama's remark, "For the first time in my adult life, I am really proud of my country." Those are just a few of the warning signs before the 2008 presidential contest that Americans should have paid more attention to. We cannot afford to do that again in 2016!

Let's analyze a piece of rhetoric from this campaign's initial Democratic presidential debate held by CNN on October 13, 2015. In that debate former Maryland Governor Martin O'Malley brought up Hillary Clinton's flip-flopping on the Iraq War by stating that she voted for the Iraq War resolution in 2002 when she was a senator and later was against the war during the 2008 presidential race — when anti-war sentiment was raging after it was discovered that Saddam Hussein did not have weapons of mass destruction. Her response was that President Obama trusted her judgment and asked her to be Secretary of State.

There was applause in the audience which highlighted that people present at the debate, and perhaps at home watching on television, liked the response. However, what does one thing have to do with the other? Whether she is right in having voted for the resolution to

9

authorize military action based on the intelligence provided to Congress by the White House at the time, and later regretted it, that has no bearing on why Obama asked her to be Secretary of State.

It would have been more appropriate for Clinton to respond by reiterating the position she has held on that matter for years: that her decision was not to go to war, but to give the president the authority to use military action if required, and that it was a vote based on the information provided at that time. Once she found out that there were no WMDs to be found, she realized (like others did as well) that she should not have voted YES.

Was the applause an approval of Hillary or of Obama's own judgments? Neither has shown the best judgment in leadership, as we shall see.

Chapter One

Lies and Deception

"Transparency and rule of law will be the touchstones of this presidency."

That was the promise made to the American people by Barack Obama when he became president. Just one day after his inauguration, President Obama wrote this memo to federal agencies: "We will work together to ensure the public trust and establish a system of transparency, public participation, and collaboration. Openness will strengthen our democracy and promote efficiency and effectiveness in Government."[3]

No doubt most Americans were delighted to hear that our new president was committed to ushering in a new era of transparency, especially when there was a level of frustration and even suspicion over the amount of information that the Bush administration was sharing with the public over events in Iraq and Afghanistan.

Obama, by promising transparency, told us that we would be able to get information on how our government was acting so that we could clearly see what was behind its actions.

How transparent has the federal government really been under President Barack Obama?

Reporters from outlets like the *New York Times*, *Washington Post*, and other mainstream news outlets have described the Obama administration as "control freak" and the "most closed they've ever covered." It should also be noted that the Obama administration has used the Espionage Act more than any other administration to prosecute reporter sources. In 2013, the Obama administration was caught spying on reporters and their parents.[4]

There are plenty of examples that illustrate how Obama had no intention of keeping his promise to give the American people a more transparent government. In fact, he promised the "most transparent government in our history." With a little more than a year remaining as of the writing of this book, Obama will leave us with a legacy of the least transparent presidency in American history.

The problem in recognizing the true lack of transparency and the blatant lies that the Obama administration emits to the American people is that the president is quite good at saying one thing for public consumption and doing another for personal political gain or for the benefit of his administration. What the president says to the American people is what the majority of the people who believe in him, certainly the majority who elected him — twice! — remember and indeed cling to. The American people must wake up and not allow themselves to be treated with the contempt with which Obama obviously regards Americans. While it may be too late now that the president is about to leave office in a year, it is not too late to make sure that we, the people who intend to responsibly elect our leaders, do a better job in the next presidential election.

We must conscientiously evaluate the candidates of both parties to avoid a repeat of past mistakes. Luckily, in the case of the likely Democratic candidate for President of the United States, Hillary Clinton, Americans have the benefit of her service as President Obama's Secretary of State most recently, and her decades of experiences as senator and first lady of the United States and Arkansas. Her experiences in those roles will certainly provide a benchmark for us to assess how she will manage the immense responsibilities of Commander in Chief.

"This is the most transparent administration in history," Obama said during a Google Plus "Fireside" Hangout.

"I can document that this is the case," he continued. That documentation was based on the procedure implemented by the administration to ensure that "every visitor that comes into the White House is now part of the public record. Every law we pass and every rule we implement we put online for everyone to see."[5]

That is the "public" comment that Obama wants the American people to remember and feel good about. After all, if the people who elected him president of the free world and once the most powerful superpower hear that his pledge to have the most transparent administration is being honored by action, they will trust his words, and rest-assured that whatever he does is for the good of the people.

It sounds quite honorable and transparent that any citizen of the United States is able to see who visits the White House. What Obama doesn't tell the American people, however, is that if members of his administration do not want a visitor to be part of the public record, they simply meet that person at a nearby café or townhouse. This is the loophole in the transparency mantra that, unless we dig deep (and who has the time to do that?), we might never know, allowing Obama to sell the American people a bill of goods he is not delivering on, and perhaps never intended to.

But that is just one simple, perhaps small, example of the deception of the American people. If we delve into the very troubling events of the "Fast and Furious" scandal, we will see the real dangers of the audacity of the hypocrisy of the Obama administration: Say one thing and do another!

We should keep in mind that the debacle of the Fast and Furious gunwalking scandal coincides with the tragedies of shootings at several of our schools, universities, and other public venues. Events that President

Obama has correctly condemned, but has hypocritically called for gun-control legislation to prevent guns from falling into the wrong hands. He simultaneously pushed for more stringent gun control and let dangerous guns and automatic weapons fall into the public domain — and not so much as take responsibility for the Fast and Furious scandal that resulted in the death of at minimum an American border patrol officer.

On October 1, 2015, after the mass shooting at a community college in Roseburg, Oregon, President Obama said:

> "Earlier this year, I answered a question in an interview by saying, "The United States of America is the one advanced nation on Earth in which we do not have sufficient common-sense gun-safety laws — even in the face of repeated mass killings." And later that day, there was a mass shooting at a movie theater in Lafayette, Louisiana. That day! Somehow this has become routine. The reporting is routine. My response here at this podium ends up being routine. The conversation in the aftermath of it. We've become numb to this.
>
> We talked about this after Columbine and Blacksburg, after Tucson, after Newtown, after Aurora, after Charleston. It cannot be this easy for somebody who wants to inflict harm on other people to get his or her hands on a gun."

However, Fast and Furious contributed some 2,000 guns and automatic weapons to the list of weapons that went into the hands of criminals.

President Obama was less than transparent and truthful with the American people during a Univision interview when he responded to interviewer Jorge Ramos, who asked Obama about the controversial Fast and Furious program, in which federal agents allowed guns to be sold and brought into Mexico so they could trace the weapons. But the U.S. Bureau of Alcohol, Tobacco, Firearms and Explosives (ATF) ended up losing track of some of the guns. Two were found at the crime scene where U.S. Border Patrol agent Brian Terry was killed on Dec. 14, 2010. The president said to Ramos:

> "I think it's important for us to understand that the Fast and Furious program was a field-initiated program begun under the previous administration. When (Attorney General) Eric Holder found out about it, he discontinued it. We assigned an inspector general to do a thorough report that was just issued, confirming that in fact Eric Holder did not know about this, that he took prompt action and the people who did initiate this were held accountable."[6]

Obama was wrong on this detail and he knew it. The purpose of his response seemed to be to protect his Attorney General, Eric Holder, rather than have his administration be accountable for this disaster — and the death of U.S. Border Patrol agent Brian Terry. Obama blatantly lied to the American people and showed a disregard for American lives which, as we will see throughout this book, has been a pattern of his administration. His legacy and his ideology, his personal agenda, were more important than any American.

The Fast and Furious program began in November 2009; ten months after Obama became president, and took place out of the Phoenix office of the Bureau of Alcohol, Tobacco, Firearms and Explosives (ATF).

Gun-buyers, many of whom the feds suspected were criminals, were permitted to take firearms purchased in the U.S. and walk into Mexico without interference from agents; the intention was that once the guns were sold to powerful drug cartels, the ATF would later trace the firearms. Whistleblowers and investigators, however, found no attempt to trace the guns.

Some ATF agents became concerned the weapons were being used for crimes. On Dec. 14, 2010, U.S. Border Patrol agent Brian Terry was killed during a gunfight. Guns in the shootout were involved in the Fast and Furious operation, it was later learned.

More than 2,000 guns were sold to suspected criminals thought to be linked to Mexican drug gangs in the two years of the operation under the Obama presidency.[7] Only 710 of those firearms were recovered as of February 2012. A number of straw purchasers have been arrested and indicted; however, as of October 2011, none of the targeted high-level cartel figures had been arrested.[8]

There was a similar operation that took place years before under the Bush administration, called "Operation Wide Receiver." It was begun in 2006 and ended in 2007. It, too, was a failed attempt to track guns. Obama, in his usual smoke-and-mirror manner of deceiving the American people, would later take advantage of this prior operation to explain his assertion that the whole operation was begun by the previous administration. That was a lie with the dual purpose of casting blame on someone else and alerting the American people that he saved the day because "When (Attorney General) Eric Holder found out about it, he discontinued it."

Guns tracked by the ATF have been found at crime scenes on both sides of the Mexico-United States border. The "gunwalking" operations became public in the aftermath of Terry's murder. Dissenting ATF agents came forward to Congress in response. According to Humberto Benítez Treviño, former Mexican Attorney General and chair of the justice committee in the Chamber of Deputies, related that firearms have been found at numerous crime scenes in Mexico where at least 150 Mexican civilians were maimed or killed. Revelations of gunwalking led to controversy in both countries, and diplomatic relations were damaged.[9]

At a shootout in 2012 between Sinaloan drug cartel members and the Mexican military where Sinaloan beauty queen Maria Susana Florez Gamez and four others were killed, authorities found another weapon, an AK-47-like WASR rifle, from the Fast and Furious operation. The Sinaloan Cartel is reported to be the largest drug trafficking gang, headed by the notorious kingpin Joaquin "El Chapo" Guzman.[10] On January 8, 2016, the Mexican military conducted a raid on a safe house in Los Mochis, Sinaloa, where El Chapo was staying. After a fierce shootout with El Chapo's bodyguards where five of his men were killed and one Marine was wounded, El Chapo and his lieutenant were captured. When the dust settled from that firefight, Mexican authorities recovered, among other weapons, a .50-caliber rifle smuggled into Mexico in the Fast and Furious operation. That type of rifle is capable of stopping a car or bringing down a small plane or helicopter.[11]

In response to an inquiry by reporters of PolitiFact Florida, who were investigating the assertion made by Barack Obama that Fast and Furious started in the previous administration, the White House said that Obama was referring to the general practice of gunwalking, which happened in both administrations. Here is where the smoke and mirrors are deployed. "The President was referring to the flawed tactic of gunwalking, which despite Republicans' efforts to politicize this issue, began under the previous administration, and it was our attorney general who ended it," is how White House spokesman Eric Schultz defended the administration. That was a lie to perpetuate the one told by President Obama.

Barack Obama and Eric Holder have never apologized to the American people for contributing approximately 1,400 illegal guns to the public domain, yet the president audaciously appears before the news media after a mass shooting to promote the need for tighter gun control.

It has been alleged by the National Rifle Association and the New American that the killing of hundreds of Mexicans and even some U.S. law enforcement officers because of the Fast and Furious program was going to be used by the Barack Obama administration as an excuse for more gun control.[12]

In the spirit of telling the American people one thing but doing something entirely different, one more example has to do with Obama's support for the release of Abdel Baset al-Megrahi, the Lockerbie bomber who was convicted in connection with the 1988 bombing of a Pan Am jet over Lockerbie, Scotland, that killed 270 people, most of them Americans. Although Obama publicly protested Scotland's decision to release Megrahi from prison and send him home to Libya in 2009, reports surfaced in the British press in July 2010 showing that the Obama administration favored the terrorist's release. For public consumption, Obama reaffirmed his position on Megrahi's release when British Prime Minister David Cameron came to visit in July 2010.

However, only a few days after Cameron departed, the British press obtained a letter that the Obama administration sent a year earlier to the Scottish government evidently indicating that it was acceptable to release Megrahi on "compassionate grounds" as long as he was kept in Scotland. The Scottish government officials, seeing that Obama had no objections to Megrahi's release, sent him back to his home country, where he lived a free man until his death in May 2012.

The families of the Lockerbie terrorist attack, learning about the letter, want to see it, but the Obama administration refuses to make the letter public. Surely, hiding its incriminating content is more important than being transparent (not to mention respectful of the victims' families) with the American people.[13]

The (Un)affordable Care Act

Americans remember quite vividly the many times that Barack Obama stood before the news media to promise the American people that "if you like your health-care plan, you can keep your health-care plan." It was a promise that served to appease the millions of Americans who already had health-care coverage and were happy with those plans and their doctors. But it was a promise that President Obama knew full well he could not keep and had no intention of keeping. In order to lend credence to his promise, he had other members of his party repeat his hollow promise.

In 2009, several top congressional Democrats echoed the president's assurances that those who were happy with their plans would be able to keep them.

Senate Majority Leader Harry Reid, the 76-year-old senator who has been in office for twenty-nine years, said the health-care overhaul effort "means making sure you can keep your family's doctor or keep your health-care plan if you like it."

Senate Majority Whip Dick Durbin told the happily insured, "We are going to put in any legislation considered by the House and Senate the protection that you, as an individual, keep the health insurance you have, if that is what you want."

And then-Senate Budget Committee Chairwoman Patty Murray also said: "If you like what you have today, that will be what you have when this legislation is passed."[14]

Anyone who called their health insurance carrier at policy renewal time and requested to keep their current plan (as promised by the President of the United States and owner of the ACA) found out that that was not possible. They were told that in order to comply with the new legislation, they had to offer a new plan with all the coverage mandatory under the new law, complete with new higher deductibles, co-pays, and premiums.

To add insult to injury, the architects of the new health-care bill, and the legislators who were responsible for reviewing and passing it, included elements of mandatory coverage that were simply absurd. We can only assume that this was done intentionally to have the insurance companies collect money from policyholders that would never be used for the prescribed coverage. That way they would have funds to cover the previously uninsured people. It was another form of redistribution of wealth, which was Obama's central purpose as president.

One such mandate was the requirement that anyone under the age of nineteen must have dental coverage. On the surface that sounds reasonable enough. That is, until parents discovered that when adding a newborn child to their policy, they were required to pay for dental coverage for their newborn. It didn't make any sense to them since it would be at least two or three years before the infant required a visit to the dentist, as recommended by pediatricians and dentists alike.

One family wrote the following letter to President Obama, hoping that he would see the flawed logic in that seemingly small part of the Affordable Care Act, and order someone to be sensible and return to the family their three hundred dollars in annual coverage per child. Here is the letter sent to the president:

January 5, 2015

President Barack Obama
The White House
1600 Pennsylvania Avenue NW
Washington, DC 20500

Dear Mr. President,

The purpose of my letter to you is to express my displeasure and confusion over one particular requirement of the Affordable Care Act. That is not to say that my family is pleased with the other parts of the law — indeed the ACA has already cost my family thousands of dollars in co-payments and deductibles. You see, Mr. President, my wife and I had a second baby in June of last year and that event has cost us approximately $6,500 in out-of-pocket medical expenses. When we had our first child three years ago prior to the ACA, our out-of-pocket cost was only a $500 deductible.

It is difficult to understand, and we cringe each time we hear your administration say, that the law is working for millions of Americans. We never hear you talk about the millions of Americans that the law is not working for. As we are Americans as well, we would like to hear more about that and what your administration plans to do about making the law more equitable for us as well. It seems that while your belief is that everyone should pay their fair share, we are paying much more than ours.

Our premiums are much higher and rising again this year. It just doesn't make sense because health care in this country is outrageously expensive. As an example, when we had our baby in June my wife spent two nights at the hospital. When we received that bill, it itemized room and board as $35,000. That did not include the doctor, the nurse, the anesthesiologist, or the nursery. Outrageous!

My point about the one particular requirement of the ACA that to us does not comport with common sense is this: When we added our newborn to our policy, forced to convert to an ACA one as we were not permitted by Horizon Blue Cross and Blue Shield to "keep our policy that we liked," we were required to add dental coverage for the newborn at an additional cost. Talk about feeling nickel and dimed by the ACA! We lobbied our carrier to remove that additional coverage, and the representative tried (she agreed that it made no sense to have dental coverage for a newborn who would not need it for at least 2-3 years), but was not allowed by her superiors. We were told it was a requirement of the ACA. My question to you, Mr. President, is why would I have dental coverage for a newborn that has no teeth, and pay the additional premium for something we will not use?

I am looking forward to your response and hopefully some common sense relief on the costs of the ACA.

Sincerely,

After a few months, a representative from the Centers for Medicare and Medicaid Services (CMS) responded to notify the frustrated family that the White House assigned the letter to them for review and resolution. Eventually, CMS responded with a letter that stated, in part:

> This is in reference to your correspondence to President Barack Obama which has been referred to my office for reply, concerning mandatory dental coverage for your newborn.
>
> The Essential Health Benefits, Actuarial Value, and Accreditation Final Regulations (published Feb. 25, 2013 at 78 Fed. Reg. 12834 - referred to as "Final Rule") requires all non-grandfathered individual and small group market plans, including qualified health plans in the Health Insurance Marketplaces, to cover all ten categories of essential health benefits (EHB). In accordance with the statute, EHB includes pediatric oral services.
>
> Notwithstanding, the Final Rule allows health insurance issuers outside of a Marketplace to exclude pediatric oral services if they have "reasonable assurance" that an enrollee has obtained coverage for pediatric oral services through a "Marketplace-certified stand-alone dental plan."
>
> As Horizon BCBS was not able to obtain such reasonable assurance from you, your newborn child was provided with a Marketplace-certified stand-alone pediatric dental plan because issuers are required under the Final rule to ensure

> *coverage for all ten categories if the essential health bene-*
> *fits.*

The official response was as ludicrous as the ACA. In true political fashion, it ignored the family's assertion that their newborn didn't have teeth, so how can it be that they had to pay for dental care? Instead, it simply recited the law.

The American people must remember that the Affordable Care Act, or the legislation more commonly known as Obamacare, was "sold" to us with the self-serving deception that, if we analyze closely, has been a hallmark of the Obama presidency: Tell the American people what they want to hear, but do otherwise.

The contempt that Obama has shown for the American people and for the country is shamelessly obvious.

Not too many people were surprised when Jonathan Gruber, a key health-care consultant to the White House and one of the architects of Obamacare, attributed the legislation's initial passage back in 2010 to the "stupidity" of American voters.[15] If Obama could deceive the American people to secure two terms of the presidency of the United States of America with his brilliantly persuasive oratory, he must have felt confident that he could do the same with Obamacare. All he had to do was "convince" all those Americans who were already insured and reasonably satisfied with their coverage that they could keep their policies and their doctors.

By the time those people figured out the blatant lie, Obamacare would be the law of the land and Barack Obama would be into his second term — securely! And all at the expense of the American people.

The epitome of Obama's hypocrisy related to Obamacare is that the only Americans who were able to keep their current health-care plans were the president, his family, and members of his administration and their families. These were the only Americans who were able to keep their coverage provided by the Federal Employee Health Benefits Program. Even members of Congress were required as of January 2014 to sign up for health coverage through Obamacare's marketplaces.[16]

America wants a leader who leads by example. It would have been more appropriate, if only symbolic, for the president to be the first American to log on to the Obamacare Marketplace on October 1, 2013, to set the example for all Americans and sign up for the First Family's new health plan through the president's Affordable Care Act. The event could have been documented by the media to display to the American people. He did not do that! The president's arrogance and disdain for the American people prevented that from being even a consideration. It was another example showing that what is good enough for all Americans is not good enough for him and his family.

Chapter Two

America Under Assault

ISIS

As of the writing of this book, the Islamic State of Syria and al-Sham (ISIS) claimed responsibility for the November 13, 2015 massacre of innocent civilians at four public venues in Paris, France. One hundred thirty people were killed and three hundred fifty-one were injured, ninety-eight of those critically. It was the largest number of deaths in France since World War II. By comparison, the 2,966 people killed in the 9/11 attacks in the U.S. by Al Qaeda, including the nineteen hijackers, was a larger number of deaths on U.S. soil than Pearl Harbor in 1941. If you ask any American, any mayor, governor, congressman or general, the United States of America, and indeed the civilized world, was at war with the Islamic extremists of Al Qaeda who carried out the 9/11 and other attacks in our homeland and abroad, and now with ISIS. Everyone, including our allies, agrees that, while this is a different war than we have been accustomed to in the past, it is nonetheless a war.

That is, all believe we are at war with radical Islamic terrorists except for President Obama. The president's refusal to see this war for what it really is — Islamic extremists' commitment to destroy America and its allies — has endangered us all, including innocent, law-abiding Muslims. Three days after the Paris attacks, ISIS announced in a new video its plans to follow up its violence in Paris with an attack in the U.S., including the Washington, DC area.

While President Bush was quick to recognize that the attacks by Al Qaeda on 9/11 were an act of war and immediately responded militarily, President Obama has been loath to do the same against ISIS. Even President Francois Hollande of France said to his people soon after the horrific attacks on innocent civilians in Paris that it was a war. "It is an act of war that was committed by a terrorist army, a jihadist army, Daesh, against France," he told the nation from the Élysée Palace, using an Arabic acronym for the Islamic State. "It is an act of war that was prepared, organized and planned from abroad, with complicity from the inside, which the investigation will help establish."

On Thursday, November 12, 2015, a day before the ISIS attacks in Paris, President Obama said in an exclusive interview with ABC News' Chief Anchor George Stephanopoulos, "The United States has been successful in containing the momentum of ISIS, but more needs to be done to completely decapitate their operations."[17] Clearly the tragic terrorist attack in Paris is a message from ISIS that they are not contained. It is a message that they are also on the move, attacking people out-side of their normal bases in Iraq and Syria.

On October 31, 2015, two weeks before the Paris at-tack, ISIS downed a Russian airliner in Egypt, killing all 224 people on board. Despite the president's rhetoric, the radical Islamic terrorists continue to inflict devas-tating harm to innocent people throughout the world. They are responsible for genocide and not contained as President Obama wants Americans to believe.

On Monday, November 16, 2015, President Obama held a news conference at the G-20 Summit in Antalya, Turkey. His reaction to the horrific massacre of so many innocent people in Paris was bizarre and trou-bling to many people, including the media asking the questions of him. Some of the reporters were obviously frustrated at the lack of urgency that President Obama showed in stepping up his so-called strategy to combat and defeat ISIS. Some in the media and in the govern-ment have repeatedly stated that the president has no viable strategy.

General Jack Keane, testifying before the Senate Armed Services Committee in May 2015, said:

> Looking at this strategy today we know now that the conceptual plan is fundamentally flawed. The resources provided to support Iraq are far from adequate. The timing and urgency to provide arms, equipment, and training is insufficient. And as such, we are not only failing, we are in fact losing

this war. Moreover, I can say with certainty, this strategy will not defeat ISIS.[18]

At the G-20 Summit, recalling that the president, in an apparent underestimation of the power of ISIS, called them a "JV" (junior varsity) team, a reporter asked him if he had underestimated ISIS. The president disputed the notion that he underestimated the Islamist terror group and said, "This is precisely why we're in Iraq as we speak and why we're operating in Syria as we speak. And it's precisely why we have mobilized sixty-five countries to go after ISIL (the acronym Obama uses to refer to the terror group)." [19]

Despite his refusal to accept that he dangerously underestimated Al Qaeda and ISIS as a direct result of his walking away from the war in Iraq (against the expert recommendations of his generals on the ground), President Obama will continue to be maligned and will be remembered for his flippant and amateurish appraisal of a rising ISIS. Here is the background:

The origin of the "JV" comment is a *New Yorker* profile of Obama by editor David Remnick published on January 27, 2014. In it, he wrote, "In the 2012 campaign, Obama spoke not only of killing Osama bin Laden; he also said that Al Qaeda had been 'decimated.' I pointed out that the flag of Al Qaeda is now flying in Fallujah, in Iraq, and among various rebel factions in Syria; Al Qaeda has asserted a presence in parts of Africa, too."

It should be noted and remembered that ISIS is an offshoot of Al Qaeda.

Obama's response: "The analogy we use around here sometimes, and I think is accurate, is if a jayvee team puts on Lakers uniforms, that doesn't make them Kobe Bryant."[20]

Obama was downplaying the seriousness of ISIS by using a sports analogy that was entirely inappropriate in the conversation. He and his administration officials had been proclaiming that Al Qaeda was decimated, so recognizing at the time that the terror group, in its original form or as a newly formed group like ISIS, was a threat that needed to be dealt with would be to effectively admit that leaving the war on terror was a mistake. President Obama is not one to admit mistakes.

At the G-20 news conference, Obama also said that he and his team understood that "this would be a long-term campaign. There will be setbacks and there will be successes. The terrible events in Paris were obviously a terrible and sickening setback." [21]

This reference to the Paris terrorist attack as being a mere setback was insensitive and outrageous, and disrespectful to those killed and injured and their families. It shows how the killing of innocent people runs counter to Obama's ideological priorities. But by downplaying the horrific killings, he again was rejecting any notion that he had made a mistake by withdrawing troops from Iraq or by declaring that he would not send American troops to Iraq or Syria to do battle with ISIS in order to ultimately defeat them.

Obama was more concerned with sticking to his plan to accept thousands of Syrian refugees into the U.S. than with altering his strategy in an effort to defeat the terrorists. He went on to say at the G-20 news conference that the attacks in Paris should not stop U.S. plans to accept refugees from Syria, many of whom are trying to flee the horrors of the Islamic State. "Slamming the door in their faces would be a betrayal of our values," Obama said. As of the writing of this book, thirty U.S. governors have called for a ban on Syrian refugees to their states.

It is entirely disingenuous for the president to attempt to appeal to Americans' ideals by suggesting that not accepting the Syrian refugees at a time when Americans are concerned about their safety and security at home would be a "betrayal of our values." Obama knows that Americans have always been an idealistic people and that we hold firmly to our beliefs of liberty, self-government, equality, individualism, diversity, and unity. It was an attempt on his part to deflect attention away from the potential dangers America faces by letting the Syrian refugees come into the country at a time when the government should be focusing on securing the homeland.

Besides, if Obama had addressed the ISIS threat directly in Syria and Iraq when it was sprouting, so many Syrian people would not have been displaced. They could have remained in their homeland, as they would have surely preferred. From July 2014 to August 2015, ISIS or ISIL (the other acronym by which it is identified, meaning The Islamic State of Iraq and the Levant) had beheaded at least 305 people, including Americans, Syrians, French, Japanese, and individuals from various other countries. ISIS also began killing and beheading Christians as it declared war on "The Cross."[22, 23] All of these atrocities occurred on President Obama's watch and after he referred to ISIS as a junior varsity team.

If the President of the United States was as concerned about the American people and keeping America safe as he is in making sure not to offend the Muslim people, everyone — Muslims and non-Muslims alike — would be much better off.

The president's inexplicable refusal to identify these groups who have openly waged war on America specifically, and western culture more generally, as radical Islamic terrorists has fostered a state of paranoia and suspicion of Muslims in general. It would be more prudent and constructive to separate the terrorists from the lawful and peaceful followers of the Islam religion. Obama refers to the ISIS and Al Qaeda terrorists as "violent extremists," when ISIS is in fact a strain of Islam, executing terror in the name of the religion.

To understand the dilemma that President Obama has engulfed western civilization in over the rise of ISIS as the new, powerful Islamist terrorist threat to the world, we should go back to his campaign promise to end the war in Iraq and Afghanistan and his ties to the Islamic world.

The president's lack of American leadership and lack of real concern for America has resulted in some of his critics calling for him to lead or resign; and referring to him as "Divider in Chief." To his credit, he is a brilliant politician. He has proven, time and again over the past seven years as president, that he has mesmerizing powers of persuasion with the American people. This is especially true with minority groups, who Obama regards as victims of American colonialism and oppression. A more appropriate title for him is Politician in Chief. As the threat of ISIS terrorism makes its inevitable impact on American soil, the president's powers of persuasion will fade along with his tenure. As more Americans lose their lives here at home at the hands of radical Islamic terrorists, more and more of the very people who supported and voted for Obama will realize that the president is not on their side.

In July 2007 then-President Bush spoke to the media from the White House briefing room on the risks of withdrawing American troops from Iraq too soon:

> "Some in Washington would like us to start leaving Iraq now. To begin withdrawing before our commanders tell us we are ready would be dangerous — for Iraq, for the region, and for the United States. It would mean surrendering the future of Iraq to Al Qaeda. It would mean we would be risking mass killings on a horrific scale. It would mean we would allow the terrorists to establish a safe haven in Iraq to replace the one they lost in Afghanistan. It would mean increas-

ing the probability that American troops would have to return at some later date to confront an enemy that is even more dangerous."

President Bush is turning out to be quite prophetic in having made that statement, but to his credit he also listened to the experts, his commanders on the ground. That is something President Obama has never been willing to do, if their recommendations run counter to his political ideology and aspirations.

As Dick Cheney, vice president under George W. Bush, and Liz Cheney wrote in their book, *Exceptional*: The cornerstone of President Obama's 2008 campaign for the presidency was his opposition to the Iraq War. One would be hard-pressed to find a single day during the campaign when Barack Obama did not promise to "end the war in Iraq." He went so far as to detail how he would carry out these plans. "On my first day in office," he repeatedly promised, "I will bring the Joint Chiefs of Staff in, and I will give them a new mission, and that is to end this war responsibly and deliberately, but decisively." The war would have to end, he said, within the next sixteen months.[24]

Those words from President Obama were the way the mission was spun to the American people. However, there was no regard for ending the war responsibly. American troops would be withdrawn deliberately and decisively, but irresponsibly. Think of President Bush's now prophetic and responsible view of what a premature withdrawal was likely to cause and the rise of ISIS. They are inextricably correlated.

In June 2015, President Obama announced that he was sending 450 more troops to Iraq to step up the training of local forces to battle ISIS. There were roughly 3,100 troops on the ground in Iraq at the time. In March 2016, the president announced that he was sending even more troops to Iraq to battle ISIS, as an ISIS attack killed one U.S. Marine, Staff Sgt. Louis F. Cardin. It is chilling to recall President George W. Bush's words.

Dick and Liz Cheney write in *Exceptional*: At his first National Security Council (NSC) meeting on January 21, 2009, President Obama instructed his military commanders to provide him with three options for withdrawal, at least one of which had to be along the sixteen-month timetable in which he had campaigned. President Obama was clearly more concerned with his ideal as the president who ended wars, not get into them. For reasons that remain unknown to most people, except perhaps the president himself, he is not interested in being Commander in Chief. He has never been in military service, yet will not heed the professional advice of his military commanders.

In response to President Obama's request for drawdown timetables, American ambassador to Iraq Ray Crocker and General Ray Odierno, the commander of U.S. forces in Iraq, recommended a period of twenty-three months before the formal end of America's combat operations. General Odierno also recommended an

American force of 50,000-55,000 troops through the end of December 2011.[25]

President Obama rejected the twenty-three-month timetable, the residual force of 50,000-55,000 through the end of 2011, and the advice that no immediate announcement on a timetable was militarily necessary.[26] The fear was that if America tipped its hand by announcing a timetable for total troop withdrawal it would only serve to embolden the terrorists.

Obama was determined to exit the war in Iraq against the Al Qaeda terrorists without an exit strategy and without regard for the potential consequences. President Obama actually aided the terrorists when he publicly announced the date for total troop withdrawal. All the terrorists had to do was wait it out, and when that date of total troop withdrawal came, they could do as they pleased. And they did! Rather than being guided by his military experts, the president opted to instead be guided by his blind arrogance.

To sell his decision to withdraw all troops from Iraq to the American people and America's international allies, President Obama lauded the "relative peace" and substantial reduction in violence in Iraq. He said, "Let me say this as plainly as I can; by August 31, 2010, our combat mission in Iraq will end." And having decided on a faster drawdown than the one recommended by his commander in the field, the president said that when the combat troops were withdrawn, he would leave 35,000-50,000 troops in Iraq until the end of

2011, after which, he explained, "I intend to remove all U.S. troops from Iraq by the end of 2011."[27] That was music to the ears of the terrorists, and planted the seed for the birth of ISIS.

Strangely, President Obama viewed walking away from a war as a victory. He did not understand that a war is won when you have defeated your enemy, and Al Qaeda was not defeated. Or perhaps it is not a lack of understanding, but a lack of willingness to fight and defeat the radical Islamists, and his personal view of America. He seems to have a belief that his destiny is to alter the entire history of the United States of America as the one country that the world looks to for leadership. That will not happen! He will leave office in one year and America will return to be the pinnacle of world leadership! Of course, it will take time for the country to recover from the damage this president has done.

It may very well be that history will view Barack Obama as more ineffectual for the prosperity of the United States of America than Jimmy Carter. Barack Obama is not likely, however, to view himself as a complete failure as president. His anti-American, anti-colonialism, and socialistic ideology are his inspiration for seeking the highest political office in the land in order to surgically diminish America's standing in the world, and he has succeeded in realizing some of those goals.

Imagine what the world would look like today if the United States had not answered the call to lead the world in defeating Hitler and the Nazis in WWII. What will the world look like five, ten, or twenty years from now if we do not lead the world in defeating Al Qaeda and ISIS? Will our allies align with Russia and Vladimir Putin to achieve that objective, as Putin continues to rebuild as much as he can of the Soviet Union while Obama is in office? We have two options: fight ISIS in their backyard or fight them in ours when they attack the American homeland.

From Dick Cheney and Liz Cheney's book *Exceptional*:

> On December 14, 2011, the president visited Fort Bragg to commemorate the end of the war in Iraq. America's withdrawal was "a moment of success," he said.
>
> Now, Iraq is not a perfect place. It has many challenges ahead. But we're leaving behind a sovereign, stable, and self-reliant Iraq, with a representative government that was elected by its people. We're building a new partnership between our nations. And we are ending a war not with a final battle but with a final march toward home.[28]

The implication being that Obama relieved Iraq of the occupation by America and that we did not influence the appointment of their new government, as America has been accused of doing in the past in other countries.

Undoubtedly, Iraq was not stable and remained fractious when Obama withdrew American troops from that country, as we have seen for several years now. And which has been confirmed by the president's unavoidable decision to send additional troops there in 2015 and 2016, as President George W. Bush predicted would be necessary.

President Obama's legacy is not yet written, but he has certainly laid the groundwork for a legacy as the president who, by leaving Iraq prematurely, gave birth to ISIS and numerous terrorist attacks that killed and injured thousands of innocent people around the world, including Americans in our homeland and abroad.

President Obama says that his number one priority is the security and safety of the American people. Certainly, it is true that that is the president's highest priority. But repeating those words without the actions to prove that America's security is well in hand is something different. At some point, the political rhetoric ceases to be effective or convincing. How valuable is American life? And do Americans believe Obama when he says that their safety and security are his primary priorities? On September 10, 2015, *The Washington Times* reported that an NBC News/ Washington Post poll showed that 47 percent of Americans felt the country was less safe than before the 9/11 attacks that brought down the World Trade Center Twin Towers. That same poll showed that only 32 percent approved of the president's handling of foreign affairs, a new low for the president.[29]

I was a bit incredulous when President Obama also said during his news conference at the G-20 Summit in Turkey on November 16, 2015, that his military advisers had told him that ground troops "would be a mistake." I knew from my research for this book that his was a history over the past seven years of his presidency of ignoring recommendations of his advisers in the field if those recommendations were contrary to his objectives and his ideals. Who are those military advisers? Let's hear from them directly their advice that troops on the ground are a mistake. And what are their recommendations for defeating ISIS?

There are numerous generals and intelligence advisers who have resigned or retired over their frustration at the president's refusal to listen to their professional advice.

Leon Panetta served as Obama's CIA director from 2009 to 2011, and then as Secretary of Defense until 2013. In his book *Worthy Fights,* he writes about part of Obama's handling of the war in Iraq, as referenced in *Newsweek* magazine:

One of Panetta's biggest criticisms concerns Obama's handling of the war in Iraq. In 2011, Panetta, along with members of the Joint Chiefs of Staff and military commanders, advocated for leaving a modest American presence to help preserve stability in a country that was on the brink of falling apart. Panetta voiced his fear "that if the country split apart or slid back into the violence that we'd seen in the years immediately following the U.S. invasion, it could become a new haven for terrorists to plot attacks against the U.S." But the administration was so eager to rid itself of the unpopular war that Obama did not actively advocate for a deal with then-Iraqi Prime Minister Nuri Kamal-al-Maliki to keep a small number of troops there. The last American troops left at the end of 2011. Panetta believes that "a small, focused U.S. troop presence in Iraq could have effectively advised the Iraqi military on how to deal with Al Qaeda's resurgence and the sectarian violence that has engulfed the country."[30]

I have always believed that direction and strategy are set at the top and then roll downhill from there. The President of the United States cannot, and the American people should not allow him to, claim ignorance or lack of knowledge. President Obama has been quick for seven years now to use that as an excuse for mishaps, and consistently blaming others. Seven years into his presidency, he is still blaming the former administration for Iraq, Afghanistan, Fast and Furious, and the economy. That is not leadership.

The former director of the Defense Intelligence Agency, and former Lieutenant General Michael Flynn, on November 24, 2015, responding to questions on the rise of ISIS, said that given the rise of ISIS and the briefs given to President Obama, "Nobody can sit here today, particularly given the amount of intelligence the

White House got and say 'We didn't know this was a problem.' Give me a break."

The former DIA director said, "Where intelligence starts and stops is at the White House. The president sets the priorities.

"The accuracy and the warnings that have been provided on the rise of radical Islamists...have been very, very clear."[31]

Chapter Three

The Refugee Crisis

The one time that President Obama demonstrated anger and disgust over the deaths by ISIS militants of the 130 innocent people in Paris was not in response to that attack (after all, that massacre was merely a setback, according to him), but rather when addressing the reaction by Americans at home who were calling for the planned migration of thousands of Syrian refugees into the country to be halted until assurances could be given that each and every refugee could be thoroughly vetted. There was a report that one of the attackers in the Paris massacre had infiltrated a group of refugees in order to make his way into France; naturally Americans were concerned that terrorists would enter the U.S. by posing as refugees.

The president's visceral disgust at Republican suggestions that his administration deny entry to refugees fleeing war-torn Syria boiled over in the Philippines Wednesday after the G-20 Summit in Turkey. Addressing reporters at an economic summit, he accused the GOP of being "scared of widows and orphans" and punctuated the upbraiding by calling the party's rhetoric a "potent recruitment tool" for the Islamic State.[32]

Although the Republican candidates vying for their party's nomination in the 2016 presidential race were calling for the president to halt the migration program, they were not the only ones. Thirty governors have also communicated with the White House their request not to accept Syrian refugees in their states. All are Republicans except for Maggie Hassan of New Hampshire, who is a Democrat.

In his usual divisive and arrogant manner, President Obama irresponsibly commented in his statement that he "cannot think of a more potent recruitment tool for ISIL than some of the rhetoric that has been coming out of here during this debate." As a leader the president has a responsibility to hear his constituents and work with the American people, including members of Congress of both political parties, to manage this, or any, crisis situation. Dictating, as Obama prefers over dialogue and negotiation, is for dictators, but it is not the American way.

The president has ignored the wishes of the American people on the life-and-death issue of safety against terror in our own home — America.

In his book *The Audacity of Hope*, Obama calls for a different brand of politics — a politics for those weary of bitter partisanship and alienated by the endless clash of armies we see in Congress and on the campaign trail; a politics rooted in faith, inclusiveness, and

nobility of spirit at the head of "our improbable exper-
iment in democracy."[33] It was not the different brand of
politics that Obama brought to the White House, despite his rhetoric. His constant and divisive attacks
against anyone, especially Congress, who disagrees
with him are insulting and beneath a level of American
leadership that the American people deserve.

Ironically, in his final State of the Union address on the
evening of January 12, 2016, President Obama lament-
ed the worsening acrimony in Washington during his
presidency. That evening he said:

"It's one of the few regrets of my presidency — that the
rancor and suspicion between the parties has gotten
worse instead of better. There's no doubt a president
with the gifts of Lincoln or Roosevelt might have better
bridged the divide, and I guarantee I'll keep trying to
be better so long as I hold this office."

The bottom line is that all Americans deserve a president, a leader, who will find a way to work with all of
the government on behalf of the people, who will show
the leadership to take responsibility for his administration, and look out for the interests of all the people of
America. It is a tall order, a difficult job, but anyone
running for the presidency of the United States of
America should know that.

President Obama is quick to conveniently forget that
the Syrian refugee crisis was sprouted from his own
indecision in the internal Syrian conflict that began in
2011. There was ample opportunity for President

Obama's administration to quell violence in Syria before it got out of hand.

In early 2011, as Obama was preparing to remove American troops from Iraq, civilian protests began in Syria against the regime of Bashar al-Assad. Launched initially in Da'ara, a town near the Jordanian border, the demonstrations quickly spread. Protesters chanted the familiar refrain that was heard in Tahrir Square in Cairo: "The people want the regime to go."[34]

The Obama administration was unwilling to do very much, despite the urging of Robert Ford, the U.S. ambassador to Syria, that Washington act to provide support for the uprisings, which were at this point largely composed of secular, peaceful groups.[35]

Assad began ordering violent crackdowns, killing protestors in an attempt to end the demonstrations. The Obama administration responded by imposing sanctions on some Syrian officials. To give support to the demonstrators, Obama announced on May 19, 2011, that if Assad was unwilling to lead the movement for reform, then it was time for him to go.[36]

Assad ignored Obama's stern words and sanctions as he stepped up his attacks on the demonstrators. Concerned that Assad might escalate his attacks on his own people by unleashing chemical weapons, President Obama, at a news conference on August 20, 2012, drew his dangerous and infamous red line:

"I have at this point not ordered military engagement in the situation... We have been very clear with the Assad regime, but also to other players on the ground, that a red line for us is we start seeing a whole bunch of chemical weapons moving around or being utilized. That would change my calculus. That would change my equation."

A year later, on August 21, 2013, Assad launched a sarin gas attack on the suburbs of Damascus where rebel groups were located. Over 1,400 civilians died. Now President Obama was forced to act as Assad crossed the red line he had drawn. The credibility of America, of the president, of the White House was at stake.

Military preparations were begun. But, according to Leon Panetta, who was Secretary of Defense at the time, "President Obama vacillated, first indicating he was prepared to order some strikes, then retreating and agreeing to submit the matter to Congress. The latter was, as he well knew, an almost certain way to scotch any action." President Obama had blinked. The consequences were devastating, as Panetta explained:[37]

When the president as commander in chief draws a red line, it is critical that he act if the line is crossed. The power of the United States rests on its word, and clear signals are important both to deter adventurism and to reassure allies that we can be counted on. Assad's action clearly defied President Obama's warning; by failing to respond, it sent the wrong message to the world.

The president's failure to act on his own warning made him, and America, look weak. It was a clear message to extremists and what eventually came to be ISIS, and to other nations, like Iran and Russia and even North Korea. They now knew that they could do as they wished and Obama did not have the military courage, will, and leadership to stand in their way.

It makes you wonder what influenced the president to display such weakness and indecision at such a critical and dangerous time in history. As he likes to say when chastising other Americans for preferring to err on the side of safety and caution over accepting Syrian refugees under porous vetting procedures, "the world was watching" as the president showed weakness.

In Barack Obama's memoir, *Dreams from My Father*, he recounts a lesson imparted by his stepfather, Lolo Soetoro. When a young Obama asks his stepfather when they were living in Indonesia if he had ever seen a man killed, the stepfather answers that he had. Obama then asks him why the man was killed. "Because he was weak," answered Lolo. "That's all?" asked Obama. Lolo's response: "That's usually enough. Men take advantage of weakness in other men. They're just like countries in that way. The strong man takes the weak man's land. He makes the weak man work his fields. If the weak man's woman is pretty, the strong man will take her. Which would you rather be?" Interestingly, Lolo then tells the young Obama, "Better to be strong. If you can't be strong, be clever and make peace with someone who's strong. But always better to be strong yourself. Always."[38]

Barack Obama would go on to become President of the United States and choose cleverness over strength in his dealings with ISIS or ISIL, Iran, Russia, and Syria. He would selectively choose strength over cleverness when dealing with Americans, including the Congress of the United States. He can show his strength at home by Executive Order.

President Obama could have avoided the current crisis of refugees fleeing their homeland in Syria if he had acted like the responsible, strong leader of the free world that he was counted on being, by America and its allies abroad. The president is just as responsible for the current humanitarian crisis as anyone else. Let's not forget the red line he had drawn as he spoke tough against Assad's brutal regime, as he chastised Americans for wanting to secure their homeland before taking in refugees from Syria.

Rather than Obama exhibiting the leadership of the President of the United States by working together with other Americans in Congress to consider ways to rationally deal with the refugee crisis, he made this contemptuous statement:

"They've been playing on fear in order to try to score political points or to advance their campaigns," Obama said of Republicans. "And it's irresponsible. And it's contrary to who we are. And it needs to stop, because the world is watching."[39] He went on to deride Republicans as being afraid of "widows and orphans." Ameri-Americans expect the president and leader to unite us in times of crisis, but Obama only knows how to divide us. That cannot stop soon enough! It is silly for the president to say that "the world is watching," when the same world has been watching and measuring the weakness and indecision he has shown over seven years as president. That, too, has to stop!

America craves nonpartisan leadership such as was exhibited by John F. Kennedy, when he said:

"Let us not seek the Republican answer or the Democratic answer, but the right answer. Let us not seek to fix the blame for the past. Let us accept our own responsibility for the future."

That is profound advice for all Americans to heed. It is advice for all the current candidates seeking to become the next president. The political party is less important than the man or woman who wants to be president. If Americans choose the individual candidate based on his or her own merits, we will do a much better job of choosing a leader. President Obama has been the most partisan leader America has had in generations, protecting his personal ideology, but not necessarily that of the Democratic Party of which he is a member.

There is a lesson in President Kennedy's words for Barack Obama, though it is contrary to his mission for America. The American people, by and large, do not care whether our leader is a Democrat or a Republican. The American people only care that the president demonstrates leadership; unite the country and be patriotic!

The past is behind us. It made no sense for the president to continuously blame his predecessor for being saddled with a mountain of problems — from the financial crisis that spawned a devastating housing crisis, severe unemployment, collapse of large corporations and countless small businesses, and near-collapse of many others. There were the wars in Iraq and Afghanistan. The American people did not need to be reminded of the root causes of these challenges. What the American people wanted and needed were for these problems to be addressed and fixed. To paraphrase JFK, the American people did not need or deserve to have a president place blame for the past, but rather to accept his responsibility to fix them and provide a better future.

President Obama did not accuse members of his own party of "popping off" when they expressed their concerns over his ineffective strategy to defeat ISIS.

Dianne Feinstein, the leading Democratic senator and the ranking Democrat on the Senate intelligence committee on November 22, 2015, said, "I don't think the approach is sufficient to the job." She also added that President Obama's decision to send fifty Special Forces to Syria will not solve the problem as she advocated a larger, more specific Special Forces operations plan. On the CBS Sunday show *Face the Nation*, she said, "We need to be aggressive now." She asserted that the United States is not doing enough to fight the Islamic state.[40] We have not yet heard Obama deride the senior senator for her comments.

On Thursday, November 19, 2015, the House of Representatives passed a bill that would suspend the program allowing Syrian and Iraqi refugees into the U.S. until key national security agencies certify they don't pose a security risk.

The vote was 289-137, with 47 Democrats joining 242 Republicans in favor of the bill, creating a majority that could override President Barack Obama's promised veto.[41] It was an overwhelming bipartisan effort to protect the American people, something the president should be interested in doing.

By threatening to veto the bill as he has said, President Obama would go directly against the wishes of the American people. According to a *Washington Post* and ABC News poll, 54 percent of Americans said they oppose taking in refugees, and 52 percent say they're not confident in the American screening process to weed out possible terrorists. The poll found that 73 percent of surveyed Americans support U.S. participation in a military operation against ISIS, and 60 percent support the use of ground forces. Fifty-nine percent of Americans said the U.S. is at war with radical Islam, and 81 percent say they anticipate a serious terror attack on U.S. soil — one of few moments since 9/11 when anxiety about another attack has reached this level.[42]

The American people deserve the benefit of the doubt from their president and leader. We should always err on the side of safety for the American people.

On December 2, 2015, two local Islamic terrorists in San Bernardino, California, killed fourteen people and wounded twenty-two others at an office holiday party where one of the terrorists worked. One of the terrorists, Tashfeen Malik, a Pakistani citizen, entered the U.S. on a fiancée K-1 visa in July 2014 with Syed Farook, who she subsequently married and had a child with. The two terrorists, who had pledged alliance to ISIS, were killed the day of the San Bernardino attack in a shootout with police.

Suddenly, President Obama's assertion that the government's vetting process of immigrants is so extensive that Americans have nothing to fear in accepting Syrian refugees was proven false, tragically. The vetting process in the case of Tashfeen Malik, who the FBI says was radicalized years before entering the U.S., was porous enough for her to get through.

Many Americans and the media often question whether President Obama is out of touch with America and the world, especially in his view and response to radical Islamic terrorism. This was made abundantly clear by the president when in a private meeting with journalists on December 15, 2015, at the White House he said that he had not realized the extent of Americans' anxiety in the wake of the Paris and San Bernardino terrorist attacks in part because he had not watched enough cable news.[43] It was a dumbfounding admission that perhaps he is not listening to his intelligence and defense advisors.

Then, to illustrate that Americans' sentiment to hold off on allowing Syrian refugees into the U.S. was justified and President Obama's indignation of that sentiment was not, on January 7, 2016, two Middle Eastern refugees were arrested in California and Texas on terror-related charges with ties to ISIS.[44]

The president may appear out of touch to many as his response to these and other events is largely unemotional and lacking in conviction. It is not due to a bright, Harvard-educated man being out of touch at all. It is simply because his view, from the very days when his desire to be a president was formed, was to reshape, indeed remake, America. The central purpose of his presidency was to level the playing field between America, the de facto superpower in the world since the end of the Cold War and the dismantling of the Soviet Union, and the rest of the world, especially the smaller nations that he believed had been stepped on by America and old world behemoths like France and Britain.

Barack Obama's motivation to reshape America in his personal image is much more complex than the simple explanation that he is out of touch with Americans. The reality is that his detachment from Americans comes from his heart being in a different place, a different land. Americans have expected something from him that he was not going to provide. If Americans truly understood Obama when he was a candidate for the greatest office in the land, they would have been sufficiently frightened not to have voted for him. But, we did not truly know Barack Obama and many still do not, though we have more clear evidence after being ruled by him for seven years now. That's right, America is being ruled instead of governed.

But now with his popularity as president in heavy decline, he seems torn between sticking to his passionate mission to knock down America a few pegs and restore the swagger that has been stifled by his failing presidency. According to a CNN/ORC poll as of January 29, 2016, 51 percent of respondents disapprove of the president's role in the Oval Office; 52 percent feel the president is leading the country down the wrong path; 62 percent believe the president is not properly countering the ISIS threat; 60 percent do not agree with his approach on Iran; and 53 percent disagree with Obama's plan to close the Guantanamo Bay prison in Cuba.[45]

Chapter Four

Afghanistan and Benghazi

Speaking about Afghanistan, Secretary of Defense Gates wrote about the deep concern he felt sitting in an NSC meeting in March 2011, listening to the president describe his determination to draw down American troops:

As I sat there, I thought: The president doesn't trust his commander, can't stand Karzai, doesn't believe in his own strategy, and doesn't consider the war to be his. For him, it's all about getting out.[46]

In another illustration of the Obama administration's attempt to deceive the American people and the world on the truthful status of the situation in Iraq and Syria, there was a report that military reports detailing the severity of the terror groups operating there were altered, effectively minimizing the strength of the groups. Two senior analysts at the U.S. military central command, CENTCOM, in September 2015 signed a written complaint sent to the Defense Department Inspector General in July alleging that the reports, some of which were briefed to President Obama, portrayed the terror groups as weaker than the analysts believed they were. The reports were changed by CENTCOM higher-ups to adhere to the administration's public line that the U.S. is winning the battle against ISIS and Al Nusra, Al Qaeda's branch in Syria, the analysts claim.[47, 48]

Whether President Obama could be accused of directly ordering the reports to be altered doesn't matter. The fact is that he had a public narrative which called for him to tell the American people that we were winning the war against Al Qaeda and ISIS, and everyone had to march in the same direction. That way the president could be "transparent" with the American people — based on the information provided to him. It didn't matter that it was false.

The president had inherited two wars in predominantly Muslim countries, Afghanistan and Iraq — wars that he loathed and wanted out of. Somehow he had the confidence that the region would rise up to complete the job the United States had begun to dismantle Al Qaeda. He still believes today that it is their responsibility locally to do that, and that America — the oppressive superpower that his ancestors and mentors taught him to loathe — should butt out. The problem he now faces, that indeed the world faces, is that if the regional countries and the many factions in Afghanistan and Iraq are not able to do that, we will be facing the consequences of increased terror networks for years, if not decades, as well as the expansion of these terror groups in Syria and Libya.

It was no coincidence that the attacks of American facilities in Benghazi, Libya, occurred on the date of September 11, 2012. It should not have been a coincidence to President Obama, Secretary of State Hillary Clinton, and U.S. Ambassador to the UN Susan Rice. Yet, in order to deceive the American people, they never focused on the fact of the date, and instead went on a public relations campaign to mislead the public through the media.

Just five days before the Benghazi attack, on September 6, 2012, as Obama accepted the Democratic Party's nomination for president and his second term, he said:

Four years ago, I promised to end the war in Iraq. We did. I promised to focus on the terrorists who actually attacked us on 9/11, and we have. We've blunted the Taliban's momentum in Afghanistan, and in 2014, our longest war will be over. A new tower rises above the New York skyline, Al Qaeda is on the path to defeat, and Obama bin Laden is dead.

It is true that bin Laden was dead, and the president deserves credit for giving the order to American Special Forces to carry out that operation. But the war in Iraq was not ended. As I have said before, a war is won when the enemy is defeated, not when you withdraw from the fight as Obama did. The tower that rises above the New York skyline is beautiful, but Obama had nothing to do with that.

President Obama was so wrong in stating that Al Qaeda was on the path to defeat that five days later, on September 11, 2012, the anniversary of 9/11, an Al Qaeda group attacked two American facilities in Benghazi, Libya, killing the United States Ambassador Chris Stevens, as well as Americans Sean Smith, Tyrone Woods, and Glen Doherty. They should be memorialized and their families respected with the truth.

In an interview with CNN's Anderson Cooper, Kate Quigley, the sister of CIA contractor Glen Doherty, one of the four Americans killed in the Benghazi terrorist attack, recalled a meeting she and her family had with Clinton at Andrews Air Force Base three days after the terrorist attack in which the then-Secretary of State said that the onslaught started as a spontaneous protest.

"She spoke to my family about how sad we should feel for the Libyan people because they're uneducated, and that breeds fear which breeds violence and leads to a protest," Quigley recalled.

But as was made clear in her November 2, 2015, testimony before Congress, Clinton knew even before the attacks were finished that terrorists with links to Al Qaeda were involved. Clinton emailed her daughter, Chelsea, stating that terrorists were involved. She relayed the same information to the president of Libya and the prime minister of Egypt in conversations in the day or two after the attack. But despite privately stating that terrorists were involved in the attack, Clinton parsed her words in public.

"When I think back now to that day and what she knew, it shows me a lot about her character that she would choose in that moment to basically perpetuate what she knew was untrue," Quigley told Cooper.[49]

Roughly two months before the presidential election, President Obama was faced with a problem. How was he going to face the American people in reaction to what appeared on television as a clear terrorist attack? He had repeatedly touted his successes against Al Qaeda, and now we had four Americans killed by the terrorist group and our embassy in Benghazi destroyed. The decision that the president made in the interest of protecting his narrative (and his upcoming re-election) that Al Qaeda had been decimated was to lie to the American people about the actual events that took place at our embassy and its annex.

Again insulting the intelligence of the American people, Obama and some of his administration officials went on a PR campaign to blame the attacks on a spontaneous uprising in response to an anti-Islamic Internet video. Obama, Secretary of State Hillary Rodham Clinton, and U.S. Ambassador to the UN Susan Rice, as well as other administration officials looked downright foolish as most Americans did not believe their assertion that the deaths of four Americans, including Ambassador Chris Stevens, were a result of a violent response to an anti-Muslim video. It was a timely and convenient excuse as the president sought re-election, even if a poor one.

There are numerous serious problems with the Obama administration's reaction to the terrorist attack in Benghazi that killed those Americans. The members of Obama's administration went out of their way from the time the attack occurred and for weeks thereafter to stress that it was in reaction to an anti-Muslim video that was posted on YouTube and which had caused violent protests in Egypt and other parts of the Middle East, even when they had clear evidence that it was a terrorist attack. Here is a rundown of the events of that fateful night of September 11, 2012, and the partial reactions that followed it:[50]

Sept. 11: The Attack

2:30 p.m. Eastern Daylight Time (8:30 p.m. Benghazi time): U.S. Ambassador to Libya Chris Stevens steps outside the consulate to say goodbye to a Turkish diplomat. There are no protesters at this time. ("Everything is calm at 8:30," a State Department official would later say at an Oct. 9 background briefing for reporters. "There's nothing unusual. There has been nothing unusual during the day at all outside.")

3 p.m.: Ambassador Stevens retires to his bedroom for the evening. (See Oct. 9 briefing.)

Approximately 3:40 p.m. A security agent at the Benghazi compound hears "loud noises" coming from the front gate and "gunfire and an explosion." A senior State Department official at the Oct. 9 briefing says that "the camera on the main gate reveals a large number of people - a large number of men, armed men, flowing into the compound."

About 4 p.m.: This is the approximate time of attack that was given to reporters at a Sept. 12 State Department background briefing. An administration official identified only as "senior administration official one" provides an official timeline of events at the consulate, but only from the time of the attack - not prior to the attack. The official says, "The compound where our office is in Benghazi began taking fire from unidentified Libyan extremists." (Six of the next seven entries in this timeline - through 8:30 p.m. EDT - all come from the Sept. 12 briefing. The exception being the 6:07 p.m. entry, which comes from Reuters.)

About 4:15 p.m.: "The attackers gained access to the compound and began firing into the main building, setting it on fire. The Libyan guard force and our mission security personnel responded. At that time, there were three people inside the building: Ambassador Stevens, one of our regional security officers, and Information Management Officer Sean Smith."

Between 4:15 p.m.-4:45 p.m.: Sean Smith is found dead.

About 4:45 p.m.: "U.S. security personnel assigned to the mission annex tried to regain the main building, but that group also took heavy fire and had to return to the mission annex."

About 5:20 p.m.: "U.S. and Libyan security personnel... regain the main building and they were able to secure it."

Around 6 p.m.: "The mission annex then came under fire itself at around 6 o'clock in the evening our time, and that continued for about two hours. It was during that time that two additional U.S. personnel were killed and two more were wounded during that ongoing attack."

6:07 p.m.: The State Department's Operations Center sends an email to the White House, Pentagon, FBI and other government agencies that said Ansar al-Sharia has claimed credit for the attack on its Facebook and Twitter accounts. (The existence of the email was not disclosed until Reuters reported it on Oct. 24.)

About 8:30 p.m.: "Libyan security forces were able to assist us in regaining control of the situation. At some point in all of this - and frankly, we do not know when - we believe that Ambassador Stevens got out of the building and was taken to a hospital in Benghazi. We do not have any information what his condition was at that time. His body was later returned to U.S. personnel at the Benghazi airport."

About 10:00 p.m.: Secretary of State Hillary Clinton issues a statement confirming that one State official was killed in an attack on the U.S. consulate in Benghazi. Her statement, which MSNBC posted at 10:32 p.m., made reference to the anti-Muslim video.

Clinton: Some have sought to justify this vicious behavior as a response to inflammatory material posted on the Internet. The United States deplores any intentional effort to denigrate the religious beliefs of others. Our commitment to religious tolerance goes back to the very beginning of our nation. But let me be clear: There is never any justification for violent acts of this kind.

11:12 p.m.: Clinton sends an email to her daughter, Chelsea, that reads: "Two of our officers were killed in Benghazi by an al Qaeda-like group: The Ambassador, whom I handpicked and a young communications officer on temporary duty w a wife and two young children. Very hard day and I fear more of the same tomorrow." (The email was discovered in 2015 by the House Select Committee on Benghazi. It is written to "Diane Reynolds," which was Chelsea Clinton's alias.)

Sept.12: Obama Labels Attack 'Act of Terror,' Not 'Terrorism'

Sept. 12: Clinton issues a statement confirming that four U.S. officials, not one, had been killed. She called it a "violent attack."

Clinton: All the Americans we lost in yesterday's attacks made the ultimate sacrifice. We condemn this vicious and violent attack that took their lives, which they had committed to helping the Libyan people reach for a better future.

Sept. 12: Clinton delivers a speech at the State Department to condemn the attack in Benghazi and to praise the victims as "heroes." She again makes reference to the anti-Muslim video in similar language.

Clinton: Some have sought to justify this vicious behavior, along with the protest that took place at our embassy in Cairo yesterday, as a response to inflammatory material posted on the Internet. America's commitment to religious tolerance goes back to the very beginning of our nation. But let me be clear - there is no justification for this, none.

Sept. 12: Obama delivers a morning speech in the Rose Garden to address the deaths of U.S. diplomats in Libya. He said, "No acts of terror will ever shake the resolve of this great nation, alter that character, or eclipse the light of the values that we stand for." He also makes reference to the anti-Muslim video when he says: "Since our founding, the United States has been a nation that respects all faiths. We reject all efforts to denigrate the religious beliefs of others. But there is absolutely no justification to this type of senseless violence. None." He uses the term "act of terror" later that night when talking about the attack at a campaign event in Las Vegas.

Sept. 12: After his Rose Garden speech, Obama tapes an interview for "60 Minutes." Obama says he didn't use the word "terrorism" in his Rose Garden speech because "it's too early to know exactly how this came about." Steve Kroft, the show's host, wonders how the attack could be described as a "mob action" since the attackers were "very heavily armed." Obama says "we're still investigating," but he suspects "folks involved in this... were looking to target Americans from the start."

Kroft: Mr. President, this morning you went out of your way to avoid the use of the word terrorism in connection with the Libya attack.

Obama: Right.

Kroft: Do you believe that this was a terrorist attack?

Obama: Well, it's too early to know exactly how this came about, what group was involved, but obviously it was an attack on Americans and we are going to be working with the Libyan government to make sure that we bring these folks to justice one way or the other.

Kroft: It's been described as a mob action. But there are reports that they were very heavily armed with grenades. That doesn't sound like your normal demonstration.

Obama: As I said, we're still investigating exactly what happened. I don't want to jump the gun on this. But you're right that this is not a situation that was exactly the same as what happened in Egypt. And my suspicion is that there are folks involved in this who were looking to target Americans from the start.

Sept. 12: Senior administration officials, who did not permit use of their names, hold a briefing with reporters to answer questions about the attack. Twice officials characterize those involved in the attack as "extremists." In one case, an official identified only as "senior administration official one" is asked by Fox News reporter Justin Fishel if the administration had ruled out the possibly that the attack was in response to the anti-Muslim video. The official says, "We just don't know."

Senior administration official one: With regard to whether there is any connection between this Internet activity and this extremist attack in Benghazi, frankly, we just don't know. We're not going to know until we have a chance to investigate. And I'm sorry that it is frustrating for you that so many of our answers are "We don't know," but they are truthful in that.

NBC's Andrea Mitchell asks officials to address news reports that the attack has been "linked to a terror attack, an organized terror attack," possibly al Qaeda. The official refers to it as a "complex attack," but says it is "too early to say who they were" and their affiliation.

Senior administration official one: Frankly, we are not in a position to speak any further to the perpetrators of this attack. It was clearly a complex attack. We're going to have to do a full investigation. We are committed to working with the Libyans both on the investigation and to ensure that we bring the perpetrators to justice. The FBI is already committed to assisting in that, but I just - we're - it's just too early to speak to who they were and if they might have been otherwise affiliated beyond Libya.

Sept. 12, 3:04 p.m.: Clinton calls then-Egyptian Prime Minister Hisham Qandil and tells him, "We know the attack in Libya had nothing to do with the film. It was a planned attack - not a protest." An account of that call was contained in an email written by State Department Public Affairs Officer Lawrence Randolph that summarizes the call between the two leaders. The email was released by the House Benghazi committee.

Sept. 12, 4:09 p.m.: At a press briefing en route to Las Vegas, White House Press Secretary Jay Carney is asked, "Does the White House believe that the attack in Benghazi was planned and premeditated?" He responds, "It's too early for us to make that judgment. I think - I know that this is being investigated, and we're working with the Libyan government to investigate the incident. So I would not want to speculate on that at this time."

Sept. 12: Libya's deputy ambassador to London, Ahmad Jibril, tells the BBC that Ansar al-Sharia was behind the attack. The little-known militant group issues a statement that says it "didn't participate as a sole entity," neither confirming nor denying the report.

Sept. 12, 6:06 p.m.: Beth Jones, the acting assistant secretary of state for the Near East, sends an email to top State Department officials that reads in part: "[T]he group that conducted the attacks, Ansar al-Sharia, is affiliated with Islamic extremists." (An excerpt of Jones' email was read by Rep. Trey Gowdy at the May 8, 2013, House oversight hearing.)

Sept. 12: Citing unnamed "U.S. government officials," Reuters reports that "the Benghazi attack may have been planned in advance" and that members of Ansar al-Sharia "may have been involved." Reuters quotes one of the U.S. officials as saying: "It bears the hallmarks of an organized attack."

Sept. 13: 'Clearly Planned' or 'Spontaneous' Attack?

Sept. 13: Clinton meets with Ali Suleiman Aujali - the Libyan ambassador to the U.S. - at a State Department event to mark the end of Ramadan. Ambassador Aujali apologizes to Clinton for what he called "this terrorist attack which took place against the American consulate in Libya." Clinton, in her remarks, does not refer to it as a terrorist attack. She condemns the anti-Muslim video, but adds that there is "never any justification for violent acts of this kind."

Clinton: Religious freedom and religious tolerance are essential to the stability of any nation, any people. Hatred and violence in the name of religion only poison the well. All people of faith and good will know that the actions of a small and savage group in Benghazi do not honor religion or God in any way. Nor do they speak for the more than one billion Muslims around the world, many of whom have shown an outpouring of support during this time.

Unfortunately, however, over the last twenty-four hours, we have also seen violence spread elsewhere. Some seek to justify this behavior as a response to inflammatory, despicable material posted on the Internet. As I said earlier today, the United States rejects both the content and the message of that video. The United States deplores any intentional effort to denigrate the religious beliefs of others. At our meeting earlier today, my colleague, the foreign minister of Morocco, said that all prophets should be respected because they are all symbols of our humanity, for all humanity.

But both of us were crystal clear in this paramount message: There is never any justification for violent acts of this kind. And we look to leaders around the world to stand up and speak out against violence, and to take steps to protect diplomatic missions from attack.

Sept. 13: At a daily press briefing, State Department spokeswoman Victoria Nuland was asked if the Benghazi attack was "purely spontaneous or was premeditated by militants." She declined to say, reiterating that the administration did not want to "jump to conclusions."

Nuland: Well, as we said yesterday when we were on background, we are very cautious about drawing any conclusions with regard to who the perpetrators were, what their motivations were, whether it was premeditated, whether they had any external contacts, whether there was any link, until we have a chance to investigate along with the Libyans. So I know that's going to be frustrating for you, but we really want to make sure that we do this right and we don't jump to conclusions.

That said, obviously, there are plenty of people around the region citing this disgusting video as something that has been motivating. As the secretary said this morning, while we as Americans, of course, respect free speech, respect free expression, there's never an excuse for it to become violent.

Sept. 13: Clinton met with Moroccan Foreign Minister Saad-Eddine Al-Othmani. She condemned what she called the "disgusting and reprehensible" anti-Muslim video and the violence that it triggered. She said, "Islam, like other religions, respects the fundamental dignity of human beings, and it is a violation of that fundamental dignity to wage attacks on innocents. As long as there are those who are willing to shed blood and take innocent life in the name of religion, the name of God, the world will never know a true and lasting peace."

Sept. 13: At a campaign event in Colorado, Obama again uses the phrase "act of terror." He says: "I want people around the world to hear me: To all those who would do us harm, no act of terror will go unpunished."

Sept. 13: CNN reports that unnamed "State Department officials" say the incident in Benghazi was a "clearly planned military-type attack" unrelated to the anti-Muslim movie.

CNN: *"It was not an innocent mob," one senior official said. "The video or 9/11 made a handy excuse and could be fortuitous from their perspective but this was a clearly planned military-type attack."*

Sept. 14: White House Says No Evidence of Planned Attack

Sept. 14: Clinton spoke at Andrews Air Force Base at a ceremony to receive the remains of those killed in Benghazi. She remarked that she received a letter from the president of the Palestinian Authority praising Stevens and "deploring - and I quote - 'an act of ugly terror.' " She, however, did not call it an act of terror or a terrorist attack and neither did the president.

Sept. 14: At a State Department press briefing, spokeswoman Nuland says the department will no longer answer any questions about the Benghazi attack. "It is now something that you need to talk to the FBI about, not to us about, because it's their investigation."

Sept. 14: At a White House press briefing, Press Secretary Carney denies reports that it was a preplanned attack. "I have seen that report, and the story is absolutely wrong. We were not aware of any actionable intelligence indicating that an attack on the U.S. mission in Benghazi was planned or imminent. That report is false." Later in that same briefing, Carney is told that Pentagon officials informed members of Congress at a closed-door meeting that the Benghazi attack was a planned terrorist attack. Carney said the matter is being investigated but White House officials "don't have and did not have concrete evidence to suggest that this was not in reaction to the film."

Question: Jay, one last question - while we were sitting here - [Defense] Secretary [Leon] Panetta and the Vice Chair of the Joint Chiefs briefed the Senate Armed Services Committee. And the senators came out and said their indication was that this, or the attack on Benghazi was a terrorist attack organized and carried out by terrorists, that it was premeditated, a calculated act of terror. Levin said - Senator Levin - I think it was a planned, premeditated attack. The kind of equipment that they had used was evidence it was a planned, premeditated attack. Is there anything more you can - now that the administration is briefing senators on this, is there anything more you can tell us?

Carney: Well, I think we wait to hear from administration officials. Again, it's actively under investigation, both the Benghazi attack and incidents elsewhere. And my point was that we don't have and did not have concrete evidence to suggest that this was not in reaction to the film. But we're obviously investigating the matter, and I'll certainly - I'm sure both the Department of Defense and the White House and other places will have more to say about that as more information becomes available.

Sept. 14: Defense Secretary Leon Panetta meets with the Senate Armed Services Committee. *Roll Call*, a Capitol Hill newspaper, reports that Republicans and Democrats came away with the conclusion that the Benghazi attack was a planned terrorist attack.

> *The Hill: Senators spoke with Panetta about the response to the situation in Libya. Four Americans were killed in an attack Tuesday on the U.S. consulate in Benghazi, including Ambassador Chris Stevens.*
>
> *Senators said it has become clearer the attack was coordinated, although they would not say anything specific about any connection to the broader protests that came after an anti-Muslim video was released.*
>
> *"I think it was a planned, premeditated attack," Senate Armed Services Chairman Carl Levin (D-Mich.) said. He added he did not know the specific group responsible for the assault on the complex.*
>
> *[Sen. John] McCain expressed a similar view.*
>
> *"People don't go to demonstrate and carry RPGs and automatic weapons," he said, adding that the facts suggest "this was not a 'mob' action [or] a group of protesters."*

Sept. 15-16: Susan Rice Contradicts Libyan President

Sept. 15: Obama discusses the Benghazi attack in his weekly address. He makes no mention of terror, terrorists or extremists. He does talk about the anti-Muslim film and "every angry mob" that it inspired in pockets of the Middle East.

Obama: This tragic attack [in Benghazi] takes place at a time of turmoil and protest in many different countries. I have made it clear that the United States has a profound respect for people of all faiths. We stand for religious freedom. And we reject the denigration of any religion - including Islam.

Yet there is never any justification for violence. There is no religion that condones the targeting of innocent men and women. There is no excuse for attacks on our embassies and consulates.

Sept. 16: Libya President Mohamed Magariaf says on CBS News' "Face the Nation" that the attack on the U.S. consulate was planned months in advance. But Susan Rice, the U.S. ambassador to the United Nations, tells CBS News' Bob Schieffer: "We do not have information at present that leads us to conclude that this was premeditated or preplanned." She says it began "spontaneously... as a reaction to what had transpired some hours earlier in Cairo," and "extremist elements" joined in the protest. (It was later learned that Rice received her information from talking points developed by the CIA.)

Update, May 16, 2013: The talking points given to Rice were extensively revised, largely at the request of the State Department. The original CIA talking points said, "We do know that Islamic extremists with ties to al-

Qa'ida participated in the attack." And they said that "[i]nitial press reporting linked the attack to Ansar al-Sharia." References to al-Qaeda and Ansar al-Sharia were removed. However, all of the drafts say the attack began "spontaneously" in response to the Cairo protest. Read our article "Benghazi Attack, Revisited" for more information on what changes were made to the talking points.

Update, May 2, 2014: Two days before Rice's appearance on the Sunday talk show circuit, Deputy National Security Adviser for Strategic Communications Ben Rhodes sent an email *to other administration officials, including White House Press Secretary Jay Carney, with the subject line "PREP CALL with Susan: Saturday at 4:00 pm ET." Rhodes' email outlined four "goals" for Rice's TV appearances. One of the goals: "To underscore that these protests are rooted in an Internet video, and not a broader failure of policy." The email contained a mock Q&A session, and the third question asked whether the Benghazi attack was "an intelligence failure." The answer in the email parroted - nearly word for word - Rice's talking points when it said: "The currently available information suggests that the demonstrations in Benghazi were spontaneously inspired by the protests at the US Embassy in Cairo and evolved into a direct assault against the US Consulate and subsequently its annex." The Rhodes email was* released April 29 by Judicial Watch, *a conservative watchdog group that obtained 41 State Department documents under the Freedom of Information Act.*

Schieffer: Was this a long-planned attack, as far as you know? Or what - what do you know about that?

Magariaf: The way these perpetrators acted and moved... this leaves us with no doubt that this was pre-planned, determined- predetermined.

Schieffer: And you believe that this was the work of al Qaeda and you believe that it was led by foreigners. Is that - is that what you are telling us?

Magariaf: It was planned - definitely, it was planned by foreigners, by people who - who entered the country a few months ago, and they were planning this criminal act since their - since their arrival...

Schieffer: And joining us now, Susan Rice, the U.N. ambassador, our U.N. ambassador. Madam Ambassador, [Magariaf] says this is something that has been in the planning stages for months. I understand you have been saying that you think it was spontaneous? Are we not on the same page here?

Rice: Bob, let me tell you what we understand to be the assessment at present. First of all, very importantly, as you discussed with the president, there is an investigation that the United States government will launch led by the FBI, that has begun and -

They are not on the ground yet, but they have already begun looking at all sorts of evidence of - of various sorts already available to them and to us. And they will get on the ground and continue the investigation. So we'll want to see the results of that investigation to draw any definitive conclusions.

But based on the best information we have to date, what our assessment is as of the present is in fact what began spontaneously in Benghazi as a reaction to what had transpired some hours earlier in Cairo where, of course, as you know, there was a violent protest outside of our embassy - sparked by this hateful video. But soon after that spontaneous protest began outside of our consulate in Benghazi, we believe that it looks like extremist elements, individuals, joined in that - in that effort with heavy weapons of the sort that are, unfortunately, readily now available in Libya post-revolution. And that it spun from there into something much, much more violent.

Schieffer: But you do not agree with him that this was something that had been plotted out several months ago?

Rice: We do not - we do not have information at present that leads us to conclude that this was premeditated or preplanned.

Schieffer: Do you agree or disagree with him that al Qaeda had some part in this?

Rice: Well, we'll have to find that out. I mean I think it's clear that there were extremist elements that joined in and escalated the violence. Whether they were al Qaeda affiliates, whether they were Libyan-based extremists or *al Qaeda itself I think is one of the things we'll have to determine.*

Sept. 16: Magariaf says in an interview with NPR: "The idea that this criminal and cowardly act was a spontaneous protest that just spun out of control is completely unfounded and preposterous. We firmly believe that this was a precalculated, preplanned attack that was carried out specifically to attack the U.S. consulate."

The complete timeline of the administration's evolving responses to the terrorist attack on the American embassy in Benghazi can be found at:

www.factcheck.org/2012/10/benghazi-timeline

Why did Secretary of State Clinton make a public statement at ten o'clock the night of 9/11/12 confirming the attack on the consulate in Benghazi and reference the anti-Muslim video, but a little over an hour later at 11:12 p.m. send an email to her daughter informing her of a terror attack in Benghazi?

The simple answer is that the administration knew that it was a terrorist attack and found it convenient two months before the 2012 presidential election to lie to the American people. There must be deeper reasons other than sheer ineptitude to motivate the president and the Secretary of State to place American lives at risk from terrorism. Their response had to be supportive of Obama's assertion that he had decimated Al Qaeda, and show that he was justified in pulling out of

Iraq. It was a reckless disregard by both Obama and Clinton for the Americans who perished that night. And to look the victims' families in the eyes and lie to them was, well, un-American.

It is deceiving, irresponsible, and insulting to the American people for the administration to quickly point to the cause of the Benghazi attack on the video, yet when questioned directly as noted in the above, make the ridiculous claim that they do not want to "jump the gun on this," as Obama said, or that they want to wait for the investigation to play out. Well, didn't they already jump the gun to call it an anti-Muslim video-motivated attack without any substantiating information?

As late as September 25, 2012, President Obama said: "That is what we saw play out in the last two weeks, as a crude and disgusting video sparked outrage throughout the Muslim world. Now I have made it clear that the United States government had nothing to do with this video and I believe its message must be rejected by all who respect our common humanity."[51]

Chapter Five

New Message to the World

As President Obama vacillated in dealing with ISIS, Al Qaeda, Assad in Syria, and Iran, Vladimir Putin in Russia was keenly observing his options to bolster his reach in Eastern Europe. Obama's message was clear to Putin and the rest of the world: Under his watch America was not interested in asserting a leadership position in the world. Indeed, Putin knew that from the first day that Obama became president of the United States and began to express his disdain for America, he had found an ally in reversing America's greatness from within. Putin and other countries interested in denting America's standing as a superpower, like Iran, waited patiently as they tested the president.

It seems that Barack Obama identified, not with America, but more with Indonesia, the nation that he called "the land of my childhood" in his 2006 book, *The Audacity of Hope*, even though he lived there only four years from six years of age to ten, after his mother married Lolo Soetoro, who would become Obama's stepfather.[52]

One of the first acts of the new president in 2009 was to embark on a world tour to inform other foreign leaders and their people that he believed that much was wrong with America and he was going to lead the United States down his version of a righteous path. In Strasbourg, France, on April 3, 2009, he said, "America has shown arrogance and been dismissive, even derisive." As he led up to his explanation on why he was closing the detention facility at Guantanamo, President Obama noted that Americans and Frenchmen had "fought and bled to uphold (our) values." He then said that Guantanamo was a "sacrifice of (our values) for expedience sake" and that was his reason for closing it.[53] The president showed a disregard for all victims of the 9/11 terrorist attack and their still-grieving families. He was more concerned with ensuring that the Al Qaeda detainees who participated in that and other terrorist attacks on Americans were treated "fairly."

President Obama refers to "our values" in an apparent attempt to persuade American and foreign listeners that his intentions are based on core American values. In fact, he was really referring to his values and his ideals - and he didn't care if Americans got hurt in the process. He was on a mission to reduce America's role on the world stage. As further clarity on his anti-American rampage on foreign soil, the president went on to explain that if America would just cut the size of its nuclear arsenal, Iran and North Korea would be convinced to abandon their nuclear ambitions. It was inconceivable for the President of the United States to fathom that those belligerent and terrorist nations like Iran and North Korea would unilaterally decide not to pursue their nuclear arms simply because America would decide to have fewer nuclear weapons of its own, when those countries seek those weapons as offensive threats and not as deterrents as the United States has done. Having nuclear weapons gives them the muscle to gain status among other nations of the world, but they have proven time and again to be hostile enough to use them if they had them.

Imagine that the president could actually believe that by weakening America, he could appease other countries and thereby somehow improve America. Absolutely astonishing!

As part of what has been referred to in the media and in books as President Obama's apology tour, in June 2009 President Obama traveled to Cairo for a speech to the Muslim world. It is worth bearing in mind that the land of his childhood was Indonesia, a nation with a Muslim population of 90 percent, anointing it the most populace Islamic-majority country. His stepfather, Lolo Soetoro, was Muslim, and Obama, under the name of Barry Soetoro, was registered in school as a Muslim. A young Barry Soetoro attended a Muslim school and later a Catholic school. At both, he was registered as a Muslim. In his autobiography, *Dreams From My Father*, Obama briefly mentions Koranic study and describes his public school, which accepted students of all religions, as "a Muslim school." Only Muslim students attended the weekly two-hour Koran class that Barry attended.

"In the Muslim school, the teacher wrote to tell my mother that I made faces during Koranic studies," Obama wrote. "My mother wasn't overly concerned. 'Be respectful,' she'd say. In the Catholic school, when it came time to pray, I would close my eyes, then peek around the room. Nothing happened. No angels descended. Just a parched old nun and 30 brown children, muttering words."[54]

Obama attended the local mosque in Jakarta for Friday prayers with his stepfather, even though he has insisted for years that he has never practiced Islam. Maya Soetoro-Ng, Obama's younger half-sister, said her father (Barack's stepfather) attended the mosque "for big communal events." Obama occasionally followed his stepfather to the mosque for Friday prayers.

Rully Dasaad, a childhood friend, said Obama sometimes went to Friday prayers at the local mosque.

"We prayed but not really seriously, just following actions done by older people in the mosque. But as kids, we loved to meet our friends and went to the mosque together and played," said Zulfin Adi, who describes himself as among Obama's closest childhood friends. "...Sometimes, when the muezzin sounded the call to prayer, Lolo and Barry would walk to the makeshift mosque together," Adi said. "His mother often went to the church, but Barry was Muslim. He went to the mosque."[55] It is worth noting that Obama's grandfather and father from Kenya were also Muslim. In *Dreams From My Father*, Obama notes his grandfather, Onyango, as a Muslim.[56]

With a significant background in Islam, despite his convenient political claims stating that he is Christian, President Obama proceeded on his trip in Cairo to acknowledge a strain between the United States and the Muslim world, as he explained, astonishingly, that the tension had been "fed by colonialism that denied rights and opportunities to many Muslims and a Cold War in which Muslim-majority countries were too often treated as proxies without regard to their own aspirations."[57]

Obama was sending a clear message to the world that he would be leading the charge to abdicate much of America's power and thereby help other countries, especially Muslim ones, elevate their political standing and their power in the interest of a planet of equal partners. It was music to the ears of the leaders of Russia, Iran, North Korea, and terrorists throughout the Middle East and all over the world. Obama's ideology and personal agenda were humiliating America, and humiliation fostered weakness.

President Obama was sending signals all over the globe that he was representing a new world order in America - his world order, and not America's. At the Summit of the Americas in Trinidad and Tobago on April 17, 2009, Nicaraguan president Daniel Ortega delivered a fifty-minute diatribe about the evil America had done in the world. Rather than dispute the distortions or cite Nicaragua's many human rights violations against its own people, including violence and rape of women and young girls, attacks on freedom of expression, and violence against protestors,[58] Obama instead gave Ortega credence by making a joke and thereby affirmed the lies. President Obama said, "I'm grateful that President Ortega didn't blame me for things that happened when I was three months old."[59] It was unbelievable that it was all about him and not about the United States of America.

Chapter Six

Here at Home

To become President of the United States in 2008, Barack Obama got the backing and the votes of 96 percent of black Americans. In 2012, that percentage was slightly less at 93 percent. The black community, along with Hispanic-Americans and the majority of the American middle class, were counting on the "Hope and Change" that Obama promised to bring to America. It was understandable as the country was in the midst of a financial crisis at home and wars in Iraq and Afghanistan. Americans were eager for change from the Bush administration.

Barack Obama seized on the country's frustration, and billing himself as somewhat of a Washington outsider (as a one-term senator and an African-American), he promised to bring hope and change to America. Most people, except for Obama and perhaps his closest confidants, expected that "Hope and Change" to be for all Americans. In reality, it was hope for a select group of people, including many in other countries, and *massive* change, not for the better, for Americans.

The Middle Class

Throughout his seven years in office, President Obama has largely ignored the middle class in America, that very group he promised to help, to bolster, when he campaigned for president in 2007 and 2008. When it comes to the economy in fact, Obama arguably has spent most of his presidency focused either on the needs of the very poor (the uninsured with Obamacare) or the very rich (Wall Street's banks and large companies like General Motors, which were nursed back to health). In his first term he used up a huge portion of his political capital on Obamacare, and very little in helping underwater middle-class mortgage holders. Nor did he effectively deploy the enormous leverage he once had over Wall Street and Main Street both to spur more lending (by providing loss-guarantees and demanding that more of the bailout funds be earmarked for loans and mortgage relief). Indeed, as economist Emmanuel Saez has written, the wealthiest one percent in the country actually made out better, in percentage terms, during Obama's "recovery" of 2009-2010 than they did from 2002-07 under George W. Bush. That might have been a non-issue if everyone else had seen wage gains as well, but everyone else did not.[60]

By 2010, a growing number of people, including African-Americans who voted for Obama in 2008, were beginning to express disappointment in the president. Americans were not seeing the progress in their own lives that was promised and were becoming impatient and disenchanted with the president. At one town hall meeting in Washington, D.C., in September 2010, Obama called on a woman who had a question for the president. The president expected a supportive embrace from the woman; after all she was an African-American and likely one of the 96 percent of black Americans who voted for him in 2008. As she began by saying that she was one of the middle-class Americans, Obama smiled in anticipation of an approving or at least a positive question - a softball that he could hit out of the park.

The smile quickly turned to a grimace as Velma Hart continued with her question, which was preceded by the expression of frustration and deep disappointment in the president - completely captured by the media for all Americans at home to see and hear. Here is what she said:

> "I'm one of your middle class Americans. And quite frankly, I'm exhausted. Exhausted of defending you, defending your administration, defending the mantle of change that I voted for. My husband and I have joked for years that we thought we were well beyond the hot dogs and beans era of our lives, but, quite frankly, it's starting to knock on our door and ring true that that might be where we're headed again, and, quite frankly, Mr. President, I need you to answer this honestly. Is this my new reality?"

In December 2015, during a focus group of Republican presidential candidate Donald Trump, conducted by the GOP political consultant and pollster Frank Lutz, an African-American, in explaining why he was supporting Donald Trump for the Republican nomination for president said that he felt President Obama was un-American. Others (white supporters of Trump), wanting to be more respectful of the president, said he was clueless, out of touch, amateurish. These are middle-class Americans who are fed up with the lack of leadership President Obama has exhibited in areas that directly impact them - the economy, jobs, and security.

Over the course of the president's two terms in office, the middle class has suffered more than at any time in America's history.

Take unemployment in America. Despite the White House, the Department of Labor, and even the media celebrating when they report the unemployment rate down to 5.6 percent as of February 2015, Americans, especially those traditionally in the middle class, are utterly confused by all the celebration. The middle class, which Obama and 2016 Democratic presidential candidate, and former Secretary of State for Obama, and former First Lady Hillary Rodham Clinton have often bandied about "saving," is not easily defined. Various economists, in an effort to adjust for the disparity in economic demographics depending on what part of the country people live in, use metrics based on either income, wealth, consumption, aspiration, and, finally, demographics.[61]

For purposes of discussion here, let us consider the income metric. Using that as a barometer for the definition of the middle class, the Pew Research Center defines the middle class as a household of four people with annual earnings of between $46,960 and $140,900.[62]

What Obama and the Department of Labor will not talk about is that if you, a family member, or anyone is unemployed and has subsequently given up on finding a job — if you are so hopelessly out of work that you've stopped looking over the past four weeks — the Department of Labor doesn't count you as unemployed. That's right. While you are as unemployed as one can possibly be, and tragically may never find work again given the drastically changing dynamics of the labor market, you are not counted in the figure we see relentlessly in the news. As of February 2015, as many as 30 million Americans are either out of work or severely underemployed. Trust me, the vast majority of them aren't throwing parties to toast "falling" unemployment.[63]

There's another reason why the official rate is misleading. Say you're an out-of-work engineer or health-care worker or construction worker or retail manager: If you perform a minimum of one hour of work in a week and are paid at least $20 — maybe someone pays you to mow their lawn — you're not officially counted as unemployed in the much-reported 5.6 percent. Few Americans know this.

Yet another figure of importance that doesn't get much press: those working part time but wanting full-time work. If you have a degree in chemistry or math and are working ten hours part time because it is all you can find — in other words, you are severely underemployed — the government doesn't count you in the 5.6 percent. Few Americans know this.

I often ask people I meet for the first time how they are doing at work. When I go to a restaurant I usually ask my waiter or waitress how long he or she has been there. That usually leads to a lively, if brief, conversation about their educational background and true aspirations. Recently, my wife and some friends visited a restaurant in Long Branch, New Jersey, on the Jersey shore. Our waiter, Bill, was pleasant and professional; some might call him "polished." It turns out that Bill graduated from the University of North Carolina with a degree in economics, but could not land a job in that field. He settled for a job as a waiter for the time being on a part-time basis. Does the Obama administration, in counting Bill as "employed," care that he is severely underemployed? I don't think so.

Coincidentally, I met another waiter, Desmond, at a different restaurant in New Jersey, with an almost identical dilemma. Desmond also graduated with a degree in economics from a local university, but has yet to find employment in his field of choice. In the meantime, he is at least earning a living as a waiter, and has a second job to help pay for student loans. He, too, is not counted as unemployed or underemployed.

None of these Americans living the scenario of Bill and Desmond feel like they are living the American dream! They could not have predicted that they would end up working jobs that did not require college degrees.

There's no other way to say this. The official unemployment rate, which cruelly overlooks the suffering of the long-term and often permanently unemployed, as well as the depressingly underemployed, amounts to a Big Lie.

And it's a lie that has consequences, because the basic part of the great American dream is to have a good job, and in recent years, America has failed to deliver that dream more than it has at any time in recent memory. A good job is an individual's primary identity, their very self-worth, their dignity — it establishes the relationship they have with their friends, community, and country. When we fail to deliver a good job that fits a citizen's talents, training, and experience, we are failing the great American dream.

Gallup defines a good job as 30+ hours per week for an organization that provides a regular paycheck. Right now, the U.S. is delivering at a staggeringly low rate of 44 percent, which is the number of full-time jobs as a percent of the adult population, eighteen years and older. We need that to be 50 percent and a bare minimum of ten million new, good jobs to replenish America's middle class.

I hear all the time that "unemployment is greatly reduced, but the people aren't feeling it." When the media, talking heads, the White House, and Wall Street start reporting the truth — the percentage of Americans in good jobs; jobs that are full time and real — then we will quit wondering why Americans aren't "feeling" something that doesn't remotely reflect the reality in their lives. And we will also quit wondering what hollowed out the middle class.

The fact is that the middle class in America has shrunk from approximately 45 million households in 2000 to 43 million in 2013. That would not necessarily be bad if those families leaving the middle class were doing so due to upward mobility, but the upper-middle class has also shrunk from 25 percent in 2000 to 22 percent of households in 2013. The only group to increase during the same period was the one in the lower tier. Those households below the middle tier increased from 31 million to 34 million households.[64]

Despite President Obama touting his glowing success in rescuing the economy and creating millions of jobs, he stands to be the only president in history not to achieve a 3 percent growth in GDP. At the current rate of growth with less than a year to the end of his presidency, Obama will be lucky to average a dismal 1.55 percent economic growth per year for his entire eight years in office.

A congressman I met with recently suggested that I be optimistic in the writing of this book, and that America is currently going through a rough patch, but we will come out of it. That may be true, but most of America is not so optimistic. People are angry, frustrated, seemingly sliding backward, and, most of all, afraid about the direction of the country for the middle class.

Another ominous fact is that the fastest growing segment of the new middle class has been households headed by seniors over sixty-five years old. That is largely because the Great Recession has forced many of these folks to defer retirement and extend their years of employment. As they finally retire, hopefully with time to enjoy a rocking chair on the porch, it is likely that they will fall out of the middle class.[65]

At the same time that the middle class has been decimated, the number of Americans falling into poverty and requiring government assistance has increased dramatically. That is no coincidence. When Obama took office in January 2009, the rate of unemployment was 7.7 percent, according to the Department of Labor. The labor participation rate - which represents the number of adult Americans who are either employed or actively looking for work - stood at 65.8 percent. In 2015, while the Obama administration gleefully cheered about an unemployment rate of 5 percent as of November 2015, the labor participation rate was at 62.5 percent. That is the lowest level of workforce participation of Americans at least sixteen years old in nearly four decades.

Of course, it does not help the nearly 100 million Americans who are unemployed, underemployed, and discouraged from looking for work and therefore not counted in the Labor Department statistics when the Obama administration cheers at the unemployment rate that these Americans are directly reducing. If all these Americans were counted, the unemployment rate would be closer to 10 percent - a more realistic number that deserves the attention of the federal government.[66, 67] If the middle class were truly a priority for Obama, he would be more truthful with the American people and address the dire economic condition facing the unemployed. I admit that it is a complex problem and neither the president nor Congress has the will or the strategy to address the problem in order to reverse the trend. But, the next president must address this on day one!

Obama has also not been particularly helpful in cutting the unemployment rate of African-Americans. The unemployment rate for blacks as of October 2015 was 9.2 percent, according to the U.S. Bureau of Labor Statistics. That is twice the rate of unemployment for whites and the highest for any group in the U.S.

The result of Obama's help to the middle class is that there are more people receiving government assistance in one of three forms. Under federal standards a family is considered dependent on welfare if more than 50 percent of its total income in a one-year period comes from one of three government assistance programs: Temporary Assistance for Needy Families (TANF), the Supplemental Nutrition Program (SNAP) (formerly food stamps), and/or Supplemental Security Income (SSI). According to the *Washington Times*,

"While total dependency on welfare has been growing, the number of Americans needing some form of federal aid to get by has skyrocketed. The latest report from the government estimates more than 23 percent of Americans lived in a family that received some form of welfare help under Mr. Obama, up 17.1 from the last year of Mr. Bush's presidency."[68]

As a continuing update: The U.S. national debt has risen now to $18.8 trillion. The one thing that Obama has made sure to do during his presidency is not to help Main Street or the middle class of America, but to add enormously to our national debt. Why would he do that if he wants to change America for the better?

In fiscal year 2008, before Obama took office, the national debt was $10 trillion. That means Obama has added a whopping $8.8 trillion in debt in seven years as of the writing of this book, more than $1 trillion per year on average. Why would he do this if he chastised Americans during the financial crisis to encourage us to live within our means? Remember when he said, "When times are tough, you tighten your belts. You don't go buying a boat when you can barely pay your mortgage. You don't blow a bunch of cash on Vegas when you're trying to save for college. You prioritize. You make tough choices?"

Dinesh D'Souza, who has written several books on Obama, wrote in *The Roots of Obama's Rage* about the effects of America's indebtedness on the world stage. D'Souza points out that economists Stephen Cohen and

Bradford DeLong believe that as a consequence of American indebtedness to the rest of the world, American influence is likely to decline. "The United States will continue to be a leader...but it will no longer be the boss."[69] Obama was clear in communicating his message to the world that America had been arrogant and derisive. The president did not believe that America should be more powerful than any other country. The decline of American influence and world leadership, through indebtedness as well as other means such as military neutralization and empowering of developing nations, was part of the "change" that he would bring to America as president.

Interestingly, while the middle class has been devastated during the past seven years and Obama continually castigates millionaires for making too much money, his personal net worth has risen 438 percent. The president's net worth as of the end of 2014 is estimated to be $7 million. It was estimated to be $1.3 million in 2007 before he became president. Also of note is that despite the president's rhetoric to close the income inequality gap in America, it has expanded the most under his watch. The *Independent Journal* reports as of 2013: Under President Obama, income inequality has increased dramatically. As reported here earlier, of the last three presidents, "the income gap didn't change overall during the Bush years, increased second most during Clinton's time, and has increased the most with only five years under Obama's belt."[70]

It is hypocritical for the president to reprimand any American for becoming rich when he is reaping the same benefits of the American dream - unless he redistributes his own wealth among the less fortunate. Then he can point to his example when asking other wealthy Americans to share theirs.

One of the fundamental values of America is the freedom to pursue a better life for you and your family. Many Americans who started out poor in this country have been able to prosper and become wealthy through hard work, education, and determination. It is this upward mobility that has historically driven many Americans. It seems that under President Obama this basic tenet of the American dream has gone by the wayside. Obama has shown a clear disdain for American wealth - as long as it is the wealth of others. Several friends of mine have said that they are seriously contemplating leaving the USA because it is no longer the land of great opportunity. They are not isolated cases.

In June 2014 *The Washington Post* reported that according to a new CNN/Opinion Research Corporation poll, just one in three people believe "most children in this country will grow up to be better off" than their parents. (A whopping 63 percent said their kids will be worse off.) Not only are those numbers stunning but they are also a stunning reversal from CNN data at the end of the last century (1999 to be exact)— when two-thirds of Americans predicted that children would grow up to have it better than their parents.

At his 2014 State of the Union Address, President Obama, the highest-level leader of the country, touched on the decline of opportunity in America by saying, "Today, after four years of economic growth, corporate profits and stock prices have rarely been higher, and those at the top have never done better. But average wages have barely budged. Inequality has deepened. Upward mobility has stalled. The cold, hard fact is that even in the midst of recovery, too many Americans are working more than ever just to get by; let alone to get ahead. And too many still aren't working at all."[71]

Yet, President Obama has not shown that fixing this problem for the benefit of the middle class in America is a priority for him. It may very well be that the president and those in his administration simply do not know how to fix the problems facing the American economy. It is a problem that requires strong and proactive business acumen. That is not a skillset of most politicians.

Back in 2002 Obama gave a speech in opposition of the impending Iraq war. In that speech he said, "What I am opposed to is a rash war...to distract us from a rise in the uninsured, a rise in the poverty rate, a drop in median income - to distract us from corporate scandals and a stock market that has just gone through its worst month since the Great Depression."[72] Two out of three of those (the poverty rate and median income) have not worked out so well even after Obama extricated us from Iraq in 2011.

Chapter Seven

Divided Loyalties

Barack Obama's ideology and political priorities can be said to be inspired and defined by three key attributes:

1. The influence of his father, Barack Obama Senior;

2. His disdain for Western colonialism; and

3. His Islamic history.

Let me begin this chapter by discussing the apparent anger of Barack Obama and the possible root cause or causes of that anger. Then I can discuss how over the past seven years of Obama's presidency, the actions he has taken (domestically and globally) have served only to make the majority of Americans frustrated with our leadership. I can then show how that frustration has evolved into anger among the people of America. It is anger that has given unprecedented momentum in the 2016 presidential campaign to a political outsider - Donald J. Trump. A candidate who is remaking the Republican party in his own image.

I believe that to understand Barack Obama's motivation for the domestic and foreign policies that are important to him as president, we have to understand both his upbringing and the mentors who influenced him as a young man and all the way up to the time he ran for President of the United States. Many people who oppose Obama's policies and the decisions he has made over the seven years that he has been in office find themselves dumbfounded. They believe that his decisions and policies are contrary to America's wishes, and the country's security and prosperity. Consequently, they find themselves describing Obama as out of touch. Some say that the president simply does not care what Americans think, that he has his own agenda. They refer to him as detached from America.

The reality is closer to the latter, with a sprinkling of the former. If Obama seems out of touch with Americans, it is because his agenda in remaking America was vastly different than what the people who voted for him interpreted or wanted. As I have said in earlier chapters, the president is masterful at telling the American people and the media one thing, then doing quite another. His skillful diversionary methods leave us spinning in confusion. I suggest that President Obama actually wants the American people to think that he is out of touch. That helps him disguise his true intentions in doing the things that he does to fulfill his inner mission, as America observes in total befuddlement.

In December 2015, after the San Bernardino terrorist attack in California which occurred two weeks after the horrific terrorist attack in Paris, France, the president said to journalists in a private meeting at the White House that he had not realized the extent of Americans' anxiety in the wake of the Paris and San Bernardino terrorist attacks in part because he had not watched enough cable news. When the media shared this with the American public, it left many scratching their heads and wondering "Is the president out of touch?" Yet, the focus on that statement and the criticism it generated deflected attention away from Obama's refusal to address radical Islamic terrorism head-on. There is no other conclusion to be drawn from that statement from the President of the United States. He has lived with us through 9/11; the averted Times Square terrorist attack; the failed airplane terrorist attack by a shoe bomber; the averted terrorist attack by an underwear bomber; and numerous others before the Paris and San Bernardino attacks that killed hundreds of innocent people combined. And the president is not aware of the level of anxiety of the American people? Impossible!

Another example that President Obama is not out of touch and is simply following his personal agenda to remake America is Obamacare. During his first year in office in 2009, while the country was in the midst of the Great Recession, with escalating unemployment and families hurting all over the country, the president focused almost exclusively on passing his Affordable Care Act. He might deal with the economic malaise of the country, but after his socialistic health-care legislation was secured. He misled Americans about the details of that legislation to avoid heavy criticism and opposition to it until he had the law passed by the democratically controlled Congress — with not one Republican voting for the bill. We must remember that part of the "change" he was bringing to America with his presidency was to unite the country and bring bipartisanship to Washington. But this was a large part of the president's socialistic agenda to have the federal government take greater control of the health-care part of our economy, which accounts for 17 percent of our total GDP, according to the World Bank.[73] He did not feel the need to reach out to Republicans with the Democrats controlling both houses of Congress. His arrogance would not permit it. Nor would his mission to redistribute wealth in the country permit him to have to negotiate with the other party's members.

Americans wonder why President Obama would release Muslim terrorists from Guantanamo Bay even when our intelligence community knows that some previously released prisoners returned to terrorist activities or are members of other groups actively carrying out attacks. If you study Obama's background you will come to the conclusion that his problem is not with the terrorists, but with America. It isn't that he condones what the terrorist groups do. Rather, his deep desire to remake America is focused on diminishing America's impact in the world. A diminished America, militarily and economically, would simultaneously enable previously oppressed, occupied nations to develop, and prevent America from having the strength to influence their direction. That determination perhaps grew from Obama's desire to achieve what his father was not able to and the son's natural and fervent aspiration to follow in his father's footsteps.

We are reminded that Barack Obama was born to a Kenyan father who was part of a Muslim family and was himself a Muslim until later in life when he became an atheist. Obama's grandfather, Hussein Onyango Obama, was a Muslim and raised his children in the Islamic faith. Obama lived in Indonesia for four years with his mother and Muslim stepfather, Lolo Soetoro, where he attended a Muslim school and attended the local mosque. Living in Indonesia he was struck by the poverty of the local people as well as the treatment of those locals by the British colonial rulers and white Americans doing business in the country. As a young boy, Obama was impacted by what he perceived as strangers, foreigners, disparaging and abusing the local people in their own homeland. In *Dreams From My Father*, he referred to Americans working in Jakarta as "ugly Americans" when writing about his mother's own view of the foreigners working in the country.

That experience, coupled with his Kenyan ancestry, the torture of his grandfather by the British, and the poverty he witnessed in those countries and the oppressive occupation of these and other countries that Obama felt western imperial powers like America,

Britain, and France had no business doing, created a burning desire in him to give something back to these countries. If elevating these countries bullied by western powers was at a cost to America, it was justified.

Soon after the horrific 9/11 terrorist attacks, Obama responded by suggesting that such a terrorist attack was the result of poverty among the attackers. On September 19, 2001, then-Senator Obama wrote:

> "The essence of this tragedy, it seems to me, derives from a fundamental absence of empathy on the part of the attackers: an inability to imagine, or connect with, the humanity and suffering of others. Such a failure of empathy, such numbness to the pain of a child or the desperation of a parent, is not innate nor, history tells us, is it unique to a particular culture, religion, or ethnicity. It may find expression in a particular brand of violence and may be channeled by particular demagogues or fanatics. Most often, though, it grows out of a climate of poverty and ignorance, helplessness and despair... [W]e will have to devote far more attention to the monumental task of raising the hopes and prospects of embittered children across the globe — children not just in the Middle East, but also in Africa, Asia, Latin America, Eastern Europe and within our own shores."

That belief was central to his long-term mission to elevate the impoverished and colonized people of the world, particularly in the Middle East and Africa. When

President Obama refuses to respond to Bashar al-Asad's crossing his red line; when he insists on pulling troops out of Iraq prematurely; when he releases dangerous prisoners from Guantanamo Bay; when he refuses to attack the Benghazi terrorists and save American lives before it is too late; when he negotiates a nuclear arms deal with Iran that will release sanctions and return over $100 billion to revive their economy; even when he makes an effort to restore American relations with communist Cuba, it is not because he is out of touch or weak. It is simply because the president feels a burning desire to compensate these people for the wrongful treatment at the hands of America. It is the least he can do to compensate them for America's "arrogance and derisiveness." It is for that central reason that Obama is opposed to any further military action by the U.S. anywhere in the world.

If you read his response above to the 9/11 attacks, you will have a good explanation of the president's own empathy for the Muslim world. Essentially, then-Senator Obama believed that the attackers who flew two commercial airplanes into the World Trade Center Twin Towers, and into the Pentagon in Washington, DC, might have done so as they developed a lack of compassion for the pain they caused so many people because they grew in "a climate of poverty and ignorance, helplessness and despair." Obama suggested that the failure for the terrorists to feel empathy and their numbness to the pain they caused was not natural to them, but rather, he insinuated, was learned, or grew, as a result of their own depressed economic upbringing. This explanation suggested that the terrorists' unfortunate and disadvantaged circumstances were to blame for the 9/11 attack that killed thousands of innocent people. It had nothing to do with radical Islamic terrorism.

But Obama did suggest there was an answer to avoid this type of tragedy in the future: "[W]e will have to devote far more attention to the monumental task of raising the hopes and prospects of embittered children across the globe — children not just in the Middle East, but also in Africa, Asia, Latin America, Eastern Europe and within our own shores."

There was quite a bit of turmoil in Obama's early life. His father, Barack Hussein Obama, Sr., a Kenyan-born citizen, was an absent father. He married Obama's white mother, Stanley Ann Dunham, in 1961, the same year that Barack H. Obama, Jr. was born. They separated when Obama, Jr. was two years old and divorced in 1964. Obama, Jr. did not see his father again until he was ten years old while he was living with his maternal grandparents in Hawaii, where his mother sent him to live and go to school while she remained in Indonesia. Obama's father visited him for one month. It would be the one and only time that Barack Obama, Jr. remembered spending time with his father before his death as a result of a car accident, which he caused while driving drunk in 1982. Here is how President Obama recalls his father:

"I only remember my father for one month my whole life, when I was ten. And it wasn't until much later in life that I realized, like, he gave me my first basketball and it was shortly thereafter that I became this basketball fanatic. And he took me to my first jazz concert and it was sort of shortly thereafter that I became really interested in jazz and music. So what it makes you realize is how much of an impact [even if it's only a month] that they have on you. But I think probably the most important thing was his absence I think contributed to me really wanting to be a good dad, you know? Because I think not having him there made me say to myself 'You know what I want to make sure my girls feel like they've got somebody they can rely on."[74]

Despite having abandoned his son, Barack Obama's father was, and still is, a major influence in his life. The father went to Harvard and so did the son. The father was an African socialist, some say a communist, and many in America believe that President Obama's policies are socialistic. From the expansion of government control under his presidency in areas such as health care with Obamacare to increasing government control of banking in the U.S. and to his mission to redistribute wealth in America (both domestically and to developing nations), Obama has given Americans reason to view that he is actually realizing his father's dreams of socialism and anti-imperialism.

Obama writes that "my fierce ambitions might have been fueled by my father — by my knowledge of his achievements and failures, by my unspoken desire to somehow earn his love, and by my resentments and anger toward him." Even in absentia, Obama confides, "My father's voice had nevertheless remained untainted, inspiring, rebuking, granting or withholding approval. You do not work hard enough, Barry. You must help in your people's struggle. Wake up, black man!"[75]

Barack was called Barry when he was a young boy and later started using his given name, Barack. His father, in telling his son that he "must help in your people's struggle," must have been referring to blacks in Kenya. It's odd that an absent father would have such a profound impact on his son, but Barack Obama, Sr. was apparently a strong-willed man and his son seems to have inherited much from him.

In *Dreams From My Father*, Barack Obama clearly tells us how he has organized his life after the ideals of his Kenyan father. "All of my life, I carried a single image of my father, one that I tried to take as my own."[76] And what was that image? It was "the father of my dreams, the man in my mother's stories, full of high-blown ideals."[77] What is of interest to people who want to know Obama is that he tells us, "It was into my father's image that I'd packed all the attributes I sought in myself." And that "I did feel that there was something to prove to my father."[78]

So, who was Barack Obama's father and what were his ideals that his son took as his own? Interestingly, in *Dreams From My Father*, Obama gives us a glimpse into who his father was, as he wants us to remember him. Obama tells us that his father lost his position in the government when he came into conflict with Jomo Kenyatta, the President of Kenya, sometime in the mid-1960s; when he tells us that his father was imprisoned for his political views by the government just prior to the end of British colonial rule; and when he tells us that the attributes of W. E. B. DuBois, Malcolm X, Martin Luther King, and Nelson Mandela were the ones he associated with his father and also the ones that he sought to instill in himself.[79] That in itself reveals quite a bit about who our president aspired to be and should explain much about whether he is out of touch, as many suggest, or simply living up to his ideals for a different America. The group whose attributes Obama "sought to instill in himself" includes a socialist black nationalist, a Muslim black nationalist, a civil rights leader, and (at the time indicated in the memoir) an imprisoned armed revolutionary.[80] That hodgepodge of attributes helped shape our president.

Of further interest is that Obama never mentions either in *Dreams From My Father* or in any of his public speeches the African socialist paper that his father authored in 1965 titled, "Problems Facing Our Socialism." It was published in the *East Africa Journal* a year after Kenyan President Mzee Jomo Kenyatta took power and the country declared independence from British rule. The theme of the Obama paper was to question, and mock, the Kenyatta government's key, controversial statement of economic policy, titled

"African Socialism and Its Applicability to Planning in Kenya." The senior Obama, who was from the Luo tribe, had a long-standing dispute with President Kenyatta, who was from the Kikuyu tribe, the largest tribe in Kenya. The Luos of Obama were the second largest.

The problem for Obama, Sr. was that Kenyatta was a leader interested in capitalism, pursuing pro-Western, anti-communist economic and foreign policies. Obama was interested in socialism and neo-colonialism and was anti-Western. The difference in ideology and political philosophies, along with the inter-tribal conflict between Kikuyus and Luos, led to Obama, Sr.'s rapid decline.

Obama's half-sister, Auma, tells him that the vice president, Odinga, who was a Luo, had said that the government was becoming corrupt. He thought that, instead of serving those who had fought for Kenya's independence, politicians had taken the place of the white colonials, buying up businesses and land that should be "redistributed" to the people. When Odinga tried to start his own political party, he was put under house arrest as a communist. Another popular Luo minister, Tom M'boya, was killed by a Kikuyu gunman. Luos began to protest in the streets, the government cracked down, and people were killed. Suspicion between the tribes grew.

As Obama says, most of the Old Man's friends just kept quiet and learned to live with the situation. But the Old Man began to speak up. His friends tried to warn him about saying such things in public, but he didn't care. When he was passed up for a promotion, he complained loudly. Word got back to Kenyatta that the Old Man was a troublemaker, and he was called in to see the president. Kenyatta said to the Old Man that because he could not keep his mouth shut, he would not work again until he had no shoes on his feet.

Auma says to Obama, "I don't know how much of these details are true. But I know that with the president as an enemy, things became very bad for the Old Man. He was banished from the government — blacklisted. None of the ministries would give him work. He began looking for work abroad and was hired to work for the African Development Bank in Addis Ababa (Ethiopia), but before he could join them, the government revoked his passport, and he couldn't even leave Kenya."

Obama tells us that finally, his father had to accept a small job with the Water Department. Even this was possible only because one of his friends pitied him. The job kept food on the table, but it was a big fall for him. The Old Man began to drink heavily, and many of the people he knew stopped coming to visit because now it was dangerous to be seen with him. They told him that maybe if he apologized, changed his attitude, he would be all right. But he refused and continued to say whatever was on his mind.[81]

Barack Obama's father was ruined by a rival tribesman who became president of Kenya; ruined by a pro-Western Kenyan leader after the country won independence from a British colonial ruler. Think about that!

It's perplexing that while Obama works to reduce America's stature in the world, he simultaneously attempts to leverage that American exceptionalism to influence other nations. Americans cannot feel good about what the President of the United States said when asked about American exceptionalism at a news conference in April 2009. Obama's response to the journalist's question was "I believe in American exceptionalism, just as I suspect that the Brits believe in British exceptionalism and the Greeks believe in Greek exceptionalism." In the second month of his presidency, the president gave America and the world the impression that our great country was nothing special after all. He marginalized our great country as being no different than Britain or Greece.[82]

With a swagger that accentuated confidence as the leader of the greatest nation on earth, and the pleasure of exhibiting that through his son, Barack Obama, Sr. had reached the heights matching, if not exceeding, his old rival Kenyatta, President Obama made an official visit to Kenya to meet with Kenyan President Uhuru Kenyatta, son of Kenya's first president, Jomo Kenyatta. At a joint press conference during that visit in July 2015, President Obama was asked by a reporter to comment on Kenya's dismal treatment of gays and lesbians.

Obama responded by saying that countries should not discriminate against people on the basis of sexual orientation. The president also said, "If you look at the history of countries around the world, when you start treating people differently, not because of any harm they're doing anybody but because they're different, that's the path whereby freedoms begin to erode."[83]

When it came time for President Kenyatta to respond, he was firm as he sent a scolding message to Obama (perhaps sending him flashes of how Kenyatta's father treated his own decades ago). Kenyatta said, "We need to speak frankly. The fact of the matter is that Kenya and the United States, we share so many values — our common love for democracy, entrepreneurship, value for families — these are things that we share. But there are some things that we must admit we don't share. Our cultures, our societies don't accept. It is very difficult for us to impose on people that which they themselves don't accept. This is why I repeatedly say that for Kenyans today the issue of gay rights is really a nonissue. We want to focus on other areas that are day-to-day living for our people — the health issues that we discussed with President Obama, these are critical, issues of inclusivity and, of women, a huge section of society that is normally left out of the mainstream of economic development, what we can do in terms of infrastructure, what we can do in terms of education, in terms of our roads, in terms of giving our people power, encouraging entrepreneurship — these are the key focuses. Maybe once, like you have, we overcome some of these challenges, we can begin looking at new ones. But as of now the fact remains that this issue is not really an issue that is on the foremost mind of Kenyans and that is a fact." It was a lengthy and firm response, reminding Obama to stay out of the affairs of Kenya and not try to impose Western ideals on its people. President Kenyatta then called on the next reporter as President Obama looked on, appearing scolded. It is worth viewing the entire press conference.[84]

Obama tried talking down to Kenyatta as he has been accustomed to doing to Americans, and this time it backfired.

The British colonization of Kenya has had a lasting and painful effect on the Obama family. It has been reported that Obama's Kenyan grandfather, Hussein Onyango Obama, was imprisoned in a detention camp in 1949 during the uprising for Kenyan independence called the Mau Mau rebellion. Some reports say that Obama's paternal grandfather was imprisoned in a high-security detention camp for two years, though Obama in *Dreams From My Father* tells us that the imprisonment was for over six months. Obama's step-grandmother tells him that when Onyango returned to their home town of Alego he was very thin and dirty. He had difficulty walking, and his head was full of lice. He was so ashamed, he refused to enter his house or tell them what happened.[85] Sarah Onyango, President Obama's grandfather's third wife, and who the president calls Granny Sarah, has said that the African warders were instructed by white soldiers to whip him every morning and evening until he confessed. The torture is said to have included squeezing Onyango's testicles with parallel metal rods and piercing his nails and buttocks with a sharp pin.[86] The family considered the British unfriendly oppressors.

Prior to Onyango's arrest by the British colonizers, he had worked for them as a cook and had taken up their customs. He gave up the local tribal attire for that of the British — trousers, shirts, and shoes. Learning of his grandfather's experiences with the British, Obama tells us in *Dreams From My Father*:

My image of Onyango, faint as it was, had always been of an autocratic man — a cruel man, perhaps. But I had also imagined him an independent man, a man of his people, opposed to white rule. There was no real basis for this image, I now realized — only the letter he had written to Gramps (Obama's white maternal grandfather) saying that he didn't want his son marrying white. That, and his Muslim faith, which in my mind had become linked with the Nation of Islam back in the States. What Granny had told us scrambled that image completely, causing ugly words to flash across my mind. Uncle Tom. Collaborator. House nigger.[87]

Obama's anger over his grandfather's imprisonment and torture at the hands of the British colonial rulers, occupiers of his family's native Kenya, would impact America's relationship with Britain during President Obama's term in the White House.

Winston Churchill was serving his second stint as prime minister of Britain when the Mau Mau rebellion was suppressed, and President Obama was keenly aware of the history and its direct impact on his family. After the 9/11 terrorist attacks in the U.S., the British government lent a bronze bust of Sir Winston Churchill to President George W. Bush as a sign of the strong relationship between America and Britain. The statue sat in the Oval Office for eight years. One of the first things that Obama did upon taking over the White House was to return the bust. He had no need for it. That was his sign to Britain, a close ally of the United States, that change had indeed come to America.[88]

Thus far we have looked into parts of President Obama's history to help explain why, contrary to the belief of many Americans, he is not at all out of touch, but rather driven by loyalties that most Americans at least have difficulty understanding. Americans expect, indeed take for granted, that our president would protect the interests of the United States; continue to cultivate strong relationships with our allies; lead the country in unifying our government and our people; and build upon the exceptional stature that America has in the world, and that the world looks upon for leadership. All of this proves to be impossible to achieve in the presence of divided loyalties.

It is important to know that President Obama was also influenced, although he and his administration do not talk about it, by his family's Muslim faith. His grandfather Hussein Onyango Obama converted from tribal religion to Catholicism and then to Islam early in life.[89] The president's father was also a Muslim and the children were raised as Muslims. One of the president's half-brothers, Abong'o Malik Obama, made some noise within the family when he built a small mosque on his property in Kenya that tourists pass on their way to visit the site of the Obama family compound. Some family members were irritated by this, thinking that the glaring symbol of the family's faith might negatively impact Obama's presidency.[90]

During the ages of six to ten, Obama lived in Jakarta, Indonesia, with his mother and stepfather, Lolo Soetoro. Lolo was also a Muslim as I have written previously in this book, and as has been vastly written about elsewhere, including in Obama's memoir, *Dreams From My Father*. In Indonesia Obama attended a Muslim school and worshiped at a local mosque with Lolo. He could not do that if he were not a Muslim. The point is that despite the Obama team telling the American people and the American media as far back as 2007 when Obama was running for president that he was not a Muslim, he has had long ties to Islam throughout his family.

These are ties that can easily influence the president's view and his actions when it comes to matters related to the Islamic faith and how America is governed.

In an early deception of the American people, Obama and his team, during the time that he was campaigning for the presidency of the United States, were dishonest in addressing his Muslim background. They knew that being a Muslim or even having a Muslim family background at that time in American history was toxic. Robert Gibbs, who was campaign communications director for President Obama's first presidential race, asserted in January 2007: "Sen. Obama has never been a Muslim, was not raised a Muslim, and is a committed Christian who attends the United Church of Christ in Chicago." But he backtracked in March 2007, asserting that Mr. Obama "has never been a practicing Muslim." By focusing on the practice as a child, the campaign is raising a nonissue, for Muslims (like Jews) do not consider practice central to religious identity. Mr. Gibbs added, according to a paraphrase by Paul Watson of the *Los Angeles Times*, that "as a child, Obama had spent time in the neighborhood's Islamic center." Clearly, "the neighborhood's Islamic center" is a euphemism for a mosque. Spending time there again points to Mr. Obama's being a Muslim.[91] This deception aided Obama in being elected President of the United States.

Once he became president, Obama was a bit more "transparent" in his support of the Muslim world, even though his loyalty to Islam, while understandable given that his family is Muslim, led him to jeopardize and even reject American principles, customs, and symbolism. We must also keep in mind that Obama's family were Shiite Muslims, which may explain his misplaced support (again, given American priorities and national security) of nations such as Iran, even over close Middle Eastern allies such as Saudi Arabia, who are predominantly Sunnis.

As president, Barack Obama would attempt to directly lift the stature of Muslim nations, while simultaneously working to diminish America's while apologizing to the world because, as he said on April 3, 2009 in France, "America has shown arrogance and been dismissive, even derisive."[92] To most Americans this was a blow to our patriotism and to our pride. It was almost as if the president was saying, "America, you have been bad, and as your new father I will have to punish you." And at the same time saying, "Muslims, Iran, all of you in GITMO, don't worry, I have your back!"

On February 2, 2010, just about one year into the Obama presidency, the chief of NASA, Charles Bolden, spoke at a press conference at the National Press Club in Washington: "When I became the NASA administrator, (President Obama) charged me with three things. One, he wanted me to help re-inspire children to want to get into science and math; he wanted me to expand our international relationships; and third, and perhaps foremost, he wanted me to find a way to reach out to the Muslim world and engage much more with dominantly Muslim nations to help them feel good about their historic contribution to science, math and engineering."[93]

Was the president detached from the American people or merely exercising an agenda based on his personal allegiance to his people in Kenya and Jakarta, and

Muslims everywhere? Regardless of the answer to that rhetorical question, the more we learn about Obama, the more we understand his process of downgrading America and elevating what Obama (and his father before his death) considered oppressed nations.

On Fox News Channel, commentator Charles Krauthammer called Bolden's comments "a new height of fatuousness. NASA was established to get America into space and to keep us there. This idea of 'to feel good about your past scientific achievements' is the worst kind of group therapy, psycho-babble, imperial condescension and adolescent diplomacy. If I didn't know that Obama had told him this, I'd demand the firing of Charles Bolden."[94]

Wonder what John F. Kennedy would think if he were alive today?

The Iran Nuclear deal that President Obama reached with the Shiite regime is of interest as well. Many in America call it the worst deal negotiated by America in the history of our great nation. Even our allies in the region, such as Saudi Arabia, Jordan, and Israel, are disappointed in it and alarmed by it. That point of view comes from the fact that President Obama and his chief negotiator, Secretary of State John Kerry, had all the leverage going into that deal and easily relinquished it. What was Obama's motivation providing the impetus for such a deal?

Perhaps it was with the hopeful aspiration of turning the Iranian regime from a foe to a friend that President

Obama sought to make a deal with Iran. Apparently, the Iranian negotiators knew quite well that in Obama they had a U.S. president who wanted to "stretch" his hand out and help them. They were well aware of his background, his Muslim family in Kenya, and his sentiments about elevating the broader Middle East. This gave them confidence that they had the upper hand in the negotiations. President Obama made it clear that he wished for Iranian-American cooperation, and they took advantage of that. It would take time, perhaps years, if ever possible, to convert Iran into a friend, but the Iran Nuclear deal could be the foundation on which to build the new and cooperative relationship, thought Obama. The only problem is that Obama has only months remaining in his presidency. The next president, regardless of political party, will likely not share the same vision or the same emotional sentiment as Obama of strengthening the Muslim nations. The next president (based on the current list of candidates) will not have the same connection to the Middle East and Africa.

The fact remains that the Iranian regime will continue sponsoring terrorism throughout the world, regardless of the deal with Obama. They will continue to disrupt the entire Middle East in an ongoing effort to gain further prominence regionally: they continue to support the Houthi Shiite rebels in the Yemen civil war; they continue their alliance with Hezbollah in Lebanon, and support Hamas in Gaza; they continue to vehemently oppose the existence of Israel and publicly commit to its annihilation. Their goal is to destabilize the entire Middle East through state-sponsored terrorism. It is naïve at best to expect them to become a friend to the United States. They may become a friend to Obama, but not to the United States.

Our longtime allies in the region are concerned that President Obama is tilting the United States away from them and onto Iran and its Shiite regime. Matt McInnis, a resident fellow at the American Enterprise Institute, said in a *U.S. News and World Report* article, "There is worry at the top of the leadership of the Gulf States that the president is not really serious about doing significant efforts to restrain Iran's activities in the region. There's a lot of mistrust and doubts with President Obama amongst Gulf leaders, so I think a lot of them are going to be waiting to see who the next president is and hope for a better relationship."[95]

Chapter Eight

Electing the Next President

In 2007 then-Senator Joe Biden made a comment about then-Senator Barack Obama and the Democratic presidential candidate that created uproar, mostly in the media. Barack Obama was the only African-American seeking the Democratic nomination for the presidency of the United States, and Biden was responding to a *New York Observer* interview when he said, "I mean, you got the first mainstream African-American who is articulate and bright and clean and a nice-looking guy. I mean, that's a storybook man." That remark was construed as racist by some. Biden apologized for the remark, stating that it was taken out of context. No one who knows Joe Biden, including prominent African-Americans like Jesse Jackson and even Barack Obama himself, interpreted the remark as racist, as the media seemed to imply that it was.[96]

It wasn't really as big a deal as the media made it out to be, but more importantly it highlighted the sensitivity with which Obama's presidential campaign was treated. It also emphasized the culture of political correctness that punishes and sometimes destroys candidates for elected office, if not adhered to. The vetting process, which usually includes the microscopic scrutiny of a candidate's history — friends, associations, public statements made on the record as well as off, contributions to organizations (financial and otherwise)— seemed to be off-limits when it came to Barack Obama.

America had its first African-American candidate who transcended color and therefore appealed to a broad segment, if not every segment, of the populace. Reading between the lines of Joe Biden's controversial statement, Barack Obama did not stand side by side with previous black presidential candidates. Obama did not speak like Jesse Jackson; he did not sound as inflammatory as Al Sharpton; and he wasn't a civil rights spokesman who was identified as aligned only with the black community.

However, if Americans and the American media had taken the time to push their way through the vapor that was Obama's seemingly inspiring oratory to seriously vet him as a candidate, they would have discovered many alarming details about him. There were plenty of details that would have raised sufficient questions to have prevented Obama from becoming president. My point is not to litigate the past, as some people correctly tell me is moot considering that Barack Obama was elected president twice, but rather to encourage the American people to bypass the rhetoric of all candidates and research their résumés and track records in determining the best-qualified candidate to lead the United States of America.

Not only was Obama not a spokesman of the civil rights movement in America like Al Sharpton and Jesse Jackson, he wasn't even a true descendant of that move-movement. His ancestors did not descend from slaves in America. He isn't even entirely black. He is biracial, as we know that his mother was a white American from Kansas and his father a black African from Kenya. He has as much a white identity as a black one. His white mother was not a descendant of slavery in America. His white maternal grandparents were not enslaved in America. His black African father and grandfather were not enslaved in America either. So, Obama's identity with blacks in America is a matter of convenience. Being perceived as an African-American provided him the convenience to position himself as America's first African-American president. He is actually America's first biracial president. Even he referred to himself in *Dreams From My Father* as a "mulatto," of mixed race.

It should not be surprising that Barack Obama himself provided the world with many clues to show that his allegiance and his attention were not with America, but with the land of his father, Kenya, and for all the lands that he considered burdened by America and other developed nations. This included the Middle East, the ancestral land of his family's Muslim faith, and Asia, the place he called "the land of my childhood" when writing about Indonesia. Why else would he say after 9/11 when he was still a senator that "the essence of this tragedy, it seems to me, derives from a fundamental absence of empathy on the part of the attackers: an inability to imagine, or connect with, the humanity and suffering of others. Such a failure of empathy, such numbness to the pain of a child or the desperation of a parent, is not innate nor, history tells us, is it unique to a particular culture, religion, or ethnicity. It may find expression in a particular brand of violence and may be channeled by particular demagogues or fanatics. Most often, though, it grows out of a climate of poverty and ignorance, helplessness and despair... [W]e will have to devote far more attention to the monumental task of raising the hopes and prospects of embittered children across the globe - children not just in the Middle East, but also in Africa, Asia, Latin America, Eastern Europe and within our own shores."

That was a clear clue and message that the 9/11 tragedy was actually not the fault of the Islamic terrorists from Al Qaeda, but somewhat America's fault for not doing more to raise the hopes and prospects of embittered children in the Middle East, Africa, Asia, and for good measure, throw in Latin America and Eastern Europe. No one questioned him on that statement or brought it up during the presidential campaign of 2008. Hillary Clinton was hesitant in attacking Obama and thereby risking alienating black voters, so she erred on the side of political correctness! That hesitation played right into Obama's hands as he gained momentum in the primaries to overtake her and win the nomination. His Republican opponents, John McCain in 2008 and Mitt Romney in 2012, likewise did not go after Obama aggressively enough to expose his background and his influences, perhaps because they, too, did not want to risk alienating black voters.

No one read his books, *The Audacity of Hope* and *Dreams From my Father*, and raised questions about other clues about Obama's intentions for America. Neither the media nor his opponent candidates asked what he meant when he said, "It was into my father's image, the black man, son of Africa, that I'd packed all the attributes I sought in myself."

America, and the media, were so enamored with Obama and the prospect of the first African-American presidential candidate who both spectrums of people, black and white, could relate to that they gave him a pass on the usual, if not obligatory, scrutiny of his past. They were giddy over the prospect of a post-racial America.

Americans should have, for the good of the country, done much more due diligence into Obama's history with anti-American individuals like his Chicago Pastor Jeremiah Wright, the man who preached "Goddamn America" as a replacement to "God Bless America." They should have questioned, indeed been alarmed by, his association with Weather Underground domestic terrorist Bill Ayers, who as an anti-Vietnam War protestor bombed federal buildings, including the Pentagon; they should have questioned him on his studies with Edward Said, Obama's teacher at Columbia University who was regarded as "Professor of

Terror" for supporting violent Palestinian resistance against what he termed Zionist colonial occupation of Muslim land; or his studies, and influence by, the Brazilian socialist Roberto Mangabeira Unger, who taught Obama at Harvard Law School and called for the "containment of American hegemony" through a coalition of China, India, Russia, and Brazil.[97]

If you believe in the proverb "Tell me who your friends are and I will tell you who you are," then all Americans should have questioned how these people, coupled with the impact his father and Kenyan family had, influenced Obama's vision for America. Or the influence of communist Frank Marshall Davis, who Obama refers to in his book *Dreams From My Father* and who was a black activist who advocated wiping out white supremacy. For a time Frank Marshall Davis was under investigation by the FBI.[98]

The point here is that as America prepares to elect a new president to succeed Barack Obama, we have to scrutinize the background and character of each candidate. For the future good of the country, Americans have to ignore all the hype, the magniloquence, the personal attacks, and focus our evaluation of each candidate on the true merits they offer and on the fundamental priorities we require to be addressed in order to restore America to the greatness we remember and enjoyed until recent times.

As Americans look to the future of this great country, and as we proceed through the nominating process of the Republican and Democratic parties in the 2016 presidential campaign, we must determine who among the candidates across both parties is likeliest to focus on restoring and building the principles and values that represent the American dream, of which all Americans, those who were born here and those who have legally emigrated here, seek restoration.

These principles and values that we must restore include the resurrection of the middle class, which has been severely damaged over the past seven years; truly overhauling the health-care system in America to reduce the cost of care for all; truly devising an immigration system to reverse illegal immigration, and develop an immigration policy that allows people seeking the American dream to emigrate here legally as long as they provide incremental value to our society, and not as an alternative labor pool that displaces Americans as a means to reduce labor costs for big corporations, and even small businesses; reform our education system at all levels, including higher education, to better prepare Americans for the transformative technologies that are redefining the economic landscape globally at internet speed; rein in the out-of-control federal government spending to reduce the U.S. national debt of $19 trillion (it has grown since the writing of this book commenced). Intertwined with these national action items is the creation of jobs so that Americans can work in capacities that they want to in order to enjoy the prosperity they always counted on being available in this great country. That includes addressing the plight of the severely underemployed, and all the Americans who have fallen out of the workforce altogether after being unable to find employment; and, finally, restoring American foreign policy to ensure our allies and those who wish us harm see that America is back.

In order for the next president to address the myriad complex issues, he or she must be, first and foremost, patriotic. The president must feel a passionate desire to restore America to greatness because of his or her emotional attachment to the country and all that it stands for, rather than despising what America stands for and therefore being committed to making it like other countries — erasing the uniqueness and grandeur of America. The president must be, and have a history of being, honest and transparent with the American people. We can ascertain these traits by delving into the past of each and every candidate. We can quite easily Google their backgrounds, speeches, writings, and interviews to determine the veracity in their behavior and analyze the judgments they have made throughout their lives. We can read their books and the reviews of those books. That is a small price to pay for every voting American, investing some time to know who we are "interviewing" to lead our country. Who can we trust to go to Washington and execute the people's business?

As of the writing of this book, there are two candidates in the Democratic Party and six in the Republican one. My guess is that by the middle of March 2016, the

Republican crowd of candidates will whittle down to three. At that time Americans can begin preparing for the general election by doing their own vetting of the remaining candidates. If nothing else, we can begin developing an informed sense of identity of each candidate who will become the nominee for each party. By the time the general election comes around, we will be much better informed and in better position to elect the best possible candidate for the country.

One thing is certain: We need new blood in the White House. We know that we do not need anyone who has a history of lying and deceiving the American people. We have had plenty of that — from the current administration and beyond. If a candidate lies to and deceives the American people, and exemplifies an aura of arrogance and elitism, he or she will abuse the privileges of the Oval Office once in power. The people should look for a healthy degree of humility in their candidate. For these reasons and more, Hillary Clinton cannot become the next President of the United States.

And here are but some reasons why not.

During the 2008 presidential campaign primaries against Barack Obama, Clinton was attempting to distinguish herself as having foreign policy credentials when referring to a trip she had taken to Tuzla, Bosnia, as first lady in 1996:

"I certainly do remember that trip to Bosnia. There was a saying around the White House that if a place was too small, too poor, or too dangerous, the president couldn't go, so send the first lady.

"I remember landing under sniper fire. There was supposed to be some kind of a greeting ceremony at the airport, but instead we just ran with our heads down to get into the vehicles to get to our base."

It turned out that her recollection of that trip was false, and she had to walk it back after she was challenged on it. The comedian Sinbad, who traveled with Clinton on that trip (he was invited to perform for American troops there), disputed her description, as did the *Washington Post.*

It must have been embarrassing to Mrs. Clinton when William Nash, who was the commander of U.S. troops in Bosnia and was at the Tuzla airport with her, spoke with Helene Cooper, diplomatic correspondent for *The New York Times.* He said there was no threat of sniper fire at the airport during her visit. He said that Mrs. Clinton was gracious during her visit and took pictures with the soldiers, but "she never had her head down. There was no sniper threat that I know of."[99]

Clinton might have thought that concocting the story would make her seem brave, willing to visit war-torn regions of the world and risking her life for America, but it resulted in questioning her honesty. That was the tip of the iceberg for her in showing the American people that she was untrustworthy and self-servingly creative at storytelling. Her judgment in underestimating Barack Obama in the 2008 race for the Democratic nomination for President of the United States, and her inability to aggressively challenge Obama to win that contest, also highlighted her suspect mettle to represent the American people in potentially tough negotiations with foreign leaders and members of Congress. If she was averse to conflict in seeking the nomination for president back then, whether innately or because she feared alienating voters who supported Obama, or was simply running a disorganized campaign, how would she be as president?

Time will tell as we progress through the 2016 nomination campaign and the general election, but Clinton's biggest strategic mistake may have been accepting the role of Barack Obama's Secretary of State. In that role Clinton was exposed, if not thrown under the bus, by her boss. Perhaps she was not as yet aware, similar to most Americans who had not delved into Obama's background as he began his first term as president in 2009, of his divided loyalties and his attachment to his father's Kenyan extreme socialistic dream and his anger at British and American colonialism. If Hillary Clinton fantasized about being her own person in carrying out the responsibilities of Secretary of State on behalf of all Americans, she was in for a surprise.

Clinton's foreign policy mission was to be based on President Obama's vision for remaking America. One can only imagine how much she wanted to go about her job as Secretary of State much differently, and how she must have questioned Obama's intentions. But there was nothing she could do. He was sternly providing the direction. Her hands were tied.

Moreover, the history between Obama and both Hillary and Bill Clinton is not one of cordiality. In fact, it is quite acrimonious. I don't think that Obama could or would forgive and forget that Hillary refused to shake his hand in 2007 on the Senate floor when he declared his candidacy for the Democratic nomination for president.[100] Or that Bill Clinton remarked to Ted Kennedy in 2008, referring to Obama as he sought the senator's endorsement for Hillary, "A few years ago, this guy would have been carrying our bags."[101] This was just one of the numerous disparaging comments made by Bill Clinton of Barack Obama during the 2008 Democratic nomination process. Still, choosing Hillary Clinton as his Secretary of State was strategic for President Obama, but not so for her.

Apparently, Hillary, in accepting the role of Secretary of State under Obama, did not remember when Obama remarked in 2007 at the final Iowa debate how he looked forward to having her advise him. The remark was said in this context:

At that debate Obama was asked how he could present himself as the candidate of change when so many of his advisers had worked in Bill Clinton's administration. As he began to respond, Hillary let out a sharp laugh and exclaimed, "I want to hear this!" Obama then responded, half in jest, perhaps, and prophetically, "Well, Hillary, I'm looking forward to you advising me as well." Obama had the last laugh, becoming her boss a little over a year later.[102]

The four years that Hillary Clinton served as Secretary of State were also damaging to her aspirations to become president in 2016. She was further exposed as dishonest and untrustworthy. Deep down Americans remember her role in the Benghazi terrorist attack that killed four of our citizens and how she lied to them (and the victims' families) about those events.

For months the evidence was mounting that the Benghazi attack was carried out by Al Qaeda and not the result of an anti-Muslim Internet video as the secretary and the administration touted, even with Al Qaeda claiming responsibility. Still, Secretary Clinton stuck to her story. Her frustration and her dishonesty level grew as she testified before the Senate Foreign Relations Committee in January 2013. She became angry when senators pressed her on what she knew and when, testily responding:

"With all due respect, the fact is we had four dead Americans. Was it because of a protest or was it because of guys out for a walk one night who decided that they'd go kill some Americans? What difference does it make?"

As Cheney wrote in *Exceptional*, this response was stunning because the alternative scenarios Secretary Clinton offered did not include what actually happened — the American facilities in Benghazi were the target of an Al Qaeda-affiliated terrorist attack. She could not bring herself to finally tell the truth, and Americans saw right through that. Equally remarkable in her angry reply was her assertion (posed as a rhetorical question) that what caused the American deaths makes no difference — when, of course, it does. How did she reconcile that with the families of Ambassador Chris Stevens and the three other Americans who lost their lives with no protection from their president and the state department under the leadership of Hillary Rodham Clinton?[103]

While the Benghazi tragedy exposed America to Hillary Clinton's lack of veracity, it certainly was not an isolated case where she could say, perhaps in the most private of conversations with her most trusted aides or confidants, that the whole video thing was Obama's doing and she could not go against the party line. There were other cases that exemplified her dishonesty.

The most serious of the issues of a lack of truthfulness and deception hanging over Clinton is her use of her own private server to host her government emails when she was Secretary of State. Her excuses for the use of a personal server to hold State Department emails that could potentially compromise sensitive information critical to national security simply do not make any sense. When the issue first arose, Clinton explained that she used a personal email address which was hosted on her own private server as a matter of convenience. In March 2015, while speaking to reporters in New York she said she used the private email server "because I thought it would be easier to carry just one device for my work and for my personal emails instead of two."[104]

She did not elicit much sympathy from the American people for that. As Secretary of State for the greatest country in the land, convenience is not a perk that is necessarily bestowed on a cabinet official. To make matters worse, we later found out that she was already carrying two devices — an iPad and a BlackBerry — while Secretary of State. It makes you think that she lied simply to hide the real motivation behind using her private server for her government emails, which gave her full control over which emails she copied to her State Department email address. Dan Metcalfe, a former head of the Justice Department's Office of Information and Privacy, said this gave her even tighter control over her emails by not involving a third party such as Google and helped prevent their disclosure by congressional subpoena. He added: "She managed successfully to insulate her official emails, categorically, from the FOIA (Freedom of Information Act), both during her tenure at State and long after her departure from it - perhaps forever," making it "a blatant circumvention of the FOIA by someone who unquestionably knows better."[105]

As Secretary of State, former senator, former candidate for President of the United States, and former first lady, she had to have known better. It seems like she counted on getting away with hiding her emails from whomever she wanted to hide them from. If she got caught, she would simply lie until the story faded away.

But it has only served to raise more questions about her trustworthiness to be president. It has become such an issue during the 2016 presidential primary campaign that the Democratic Party is whispering about Joe Biden jumping into the presidential fray should Clinton become unelectable, either due to a Justice Department indictment over her emails or because she loses significant ground to Bernie Sanders in the primaries. The bottom line is that the majority of voters consider Clinton dishonest and untrustworthy.

A Quinnipiac poll released in December 2015 showed that 60 percent of voters nationally do not consider Clinton honest and trustworthy. By contrast, 59 percent of voters consider her rival, Bernie Sanders, as trustworthy. The fear in the Democratic Party is that such a figure makes her unelectable in the general election. Clinton did not help matters in trying to assure the American public that they could trust her during a CBS interview with Scott Pelley on February 18, 2016. When Pelley pressed her on her truthfulness and asked her if she has always told the truth, Clinton responded (unconvincingly), "I've always tried to. Always. Always." Pressed further by Pelley, she seemed aggravated and responded with: "Well, but, you know, you're asking me to say, 'Have I ever?' I don't believe I ever have. I don't believe I ever have. I don't believe I ever will. I'm gonna do the best I can to level with the American people." Wow, Hillary Rodham Clinton will do the best she can not to lie to the American people![106]

The fact is that she could not say "No!" because her track record is obvious. She has blatantly lied to the American people throughout her career as a politician. Had she answered no to Scott Pelley, she would have been lying again.

Another problem we have to resolve in America, and that Clinton is not the right person to remedy, is the level of divisiveness that has grown throughout the Obama administration. This level of disunity is rampant in our federal government; it is within political parties in Congress as Republicans and Democrats have absolutely paralyzed Congress's ability to function; it is a division that has existed from day one of Obama's administration, as the president refused to engage with Republicans in Congress on any legislation, especially Obamacare, because at the time Democrats controlled both houses of Congress. It has grown more rancorous as the president takes advantage of every moment before the media to bash and denigrate Republicans in Congress. He has been condescending and highly disrespectful.

If that results in endearing some Americans to the president, it is not reflected in his popularity ratings. The American people deserve better leadership than a president who mocks and insults another branch of government simply to deflect attention from himself for inept policies. In 2011 while speaking about immigration reform at the US-Mexican border, he said: "We have gone above and beyond what was requested by the very Republicans who said they supported broader reform as long as we got serious about enforcement. But even though we've answered these concerns, I gotta say I suspect there are still going to be some who are trying to move the goal posts on us one more time.

"Maybe they'll need a moat," Obama said mockingly to laughter from the supportive crowd. "Maybe they'll want alligators in the moat." It was patronizing, disrespectful, and not the way to win friends and influence people.[107]

The vicious disunity in the country has spilled over into America's streets, as cities from Ferguson, MO, to Baltimore, MD, and elsewhere have seen their black citizens riot in the streets against police, with little or no effort from the administration to diffuse the tension. These tragic events are eerily reminiscent of the racial tensions of the sixties.

The point here is that we must have a new president who has the personality, character, and integrity to unify America at every level - from the halls of Congress, to the streets of our cities, and everywhere in between.

In October 2015, during a Democratic debate the candidates were asked which enemies they are most proud of having. It was an odd question because why would anyone be proud of having an enemy? Nonetheless, the candidates took the bait and gave their obligatory response. Hillary Clinton, when her turn came to respond, rattled off among her enemies the NRA, the health and insurance companies, and then, with a big, proud grin, added: "probably the Republicans."

With the knowledge as proud Americans that we, the people, want our full government to work together for a common cause of making America great and prosperous for every citizen, that response underscored why we could not have Hillary Clinton as our next president. America does not need, and cannot afford, another divider as leader.

Vice President Joe Biden, who spent thirty-six years in Congress as a senator from Delaware before becoming V.P. under President Obama, said it best when in response to Clinton's comment he replied:

"I really respect the members up there and I still have a lot of Republican friends. I don't think my chief enemy is the Republican Party. This is a matter of making things work."

What Joe Biden said is precisely correct! It is a matter of making things work. That is the leadership that America needs in our next president.[108]

The American people, dismayed with the Hope and Change slogan of Obama that has not materialized into the change for the better for many of them, are gravitating to a new slogan - Make America Great Again! You might say that the people had placed high expectations on President Obama and have seen those expectations dashed as many Americans are unable to make ends meet. The U.S. economic collapse of 2008 during

George W. Bush's presidency damaged many Americans. By 2016, after nearly eight years of Obama's presidency, the anxiety of the crash still has not dissipated. The economic malaise has convinced many that our federal government, from President Obama to Congress, is a system run by the Washington establishment or "insiders" and is in dire need of upheaval in order to return the government to the people. It has fermented a new American Revolution centered on reshaping the leadership in the White House.

Americans' anger began to manifest in 2009 and 2010 when a message was sent to Washington with the rise of the tea party that the people were going to take back the government by electing anti-establishment outsiders to Congress. People were growing increasingly angry at Washington's inept ability to grow the economy and produce jobs for the many who were unemployed and underemployed. Compounding people's seething anger over their own economic stagnation was a growing fear over safety at home in the wake of the Paris and San Bernardino terrorist attacks. By the time the 2016 presidential campaign season rolled around, people were angry, frustrated, and disillusioned with America's leaders. The people were prime for an outsider to come on the scene in hopes of fixing the problems they faced. While in 2008 Americans were hopeful that President Obama was the answer, by 2015 he succeeded in opening the White House door to a different brand of presidential candidate.

Jobs are front and center on people's minds. The Americans who have fallen out of the workforce, and thus not even counted among the unemployed, are tired of seeing jobs filled by illegal immigrants at the low end and by H-1B visa holders on the upper end in technology jobs; or hearing of the ranks of the unemployed growing as big corporations continue to replace U.S. workers by outsourcing more jobs offshore to India or relocating whole manufacturing plants to Mexico. It is entirely understandable why American workers feel betrayed by the government and want the next president to be someone who they believe will take up their cause.

An unemployed American drives by their local suburban train station and sees no fewer than twenty illegal immigrants lined up, waiting for a job for the day or longer. A few might be picked up by the owner of a landscaping company, or a local builder, or even a national one, eager to reduce costs and increase profits by hiring these migrants to hammer in a frame to a new home, lay roof shingles, or nail in floorboards - the stuff that can be done with low risk and does not require a state license like that required for plumbing or electrical work; or it could be a restaurant looking to hire a dishwasher or a busboy, or several of them. They don't speak English for the most part, except for the little they have picked up doing day jobs or short projects in the past. That doesn't matter. The boss will teach them all they need to know, even if it is by hand signals or by having another staff person who is bilingual translate orders. Eventually, they will learn enough to fend for themselves as they perform their jobs.

The risk of difficult communication in English is one the boss is willing to deal with in exchange for paying lower wages than if he had to hire an American. And since the cost to the consumer does not include passing on this reduced labor cost, there is more profit for the boss — an encouraging incentive. For the migrant laborer it is a win as well.

Back home, whether in Mexico, Guatemala, El Salvador, Honduras, or elsewhere, one of these young, or older, men and women might earn, if lucky enough to find work, the equivalent of $200 per month. In Mexico, adjusting for the current exchange rate of eighteen pesos to the dollar, that equates to a local salary of $3,600 pesos — per month! Chances are that the migrants who succeed in making their way across our borders to find work are more likely to make less than $3,600 pesos per month back home. Even if they make $25 per day, sometimes $50 per day in the U.S., they can make more money in less than two weeks than they were accustomed to earning back home in an entire month. That often results in the doubling and tripling of earnings, often tax free.

That is just the tip of the iceberg of our country's illegal immigration problem. The fact is that without a real effort to reverse the horrible effects of poverty in countries like Mexico, it is difficult to expect that poor people will not sneak across our porous borders in search of a better life. According to the federal government there are 11 to 12 million illegal immigrants living in the U.S. Some believe that the number is much higher than that and closer to 20 million. In 2003, the Department of Homeland Security estimated (I don't know how, if the people were undocumented) that there were anywhere from 8 to 12 million illegal aliens living in the country and that 700,000 new illegals enter the U.S. each year and reside here. If that estimate is accurate, then in 2016 we would have approximately 16 million illegal aliens on the low end and 20 million on the higher end.[109]

There are a number of ways that illegal aliens make it to the United States and settle here almost unnoticed by immigration law enforcement. While the political rhetoric centers on our porous border with Mexico (and indeed the majority of the illegal migration comes through that route), another gaping hole in the immigration system is the inability to track people who come here on tourist visas with every intention of gaming the system to remain here permanently, working at jobs that should go to Americans, or syphoning off U.S. taxpayers' dollars by taking advantage of government assistance.

Millions of illegal immigrants, whether border crosses or tourist visa violators, pay fees to fraudulent document dealers to obtain false Social Security cards, driver's licenses, even phony green cards. Often the Social Security cards are of dead Americans or newborn infants, as the Social Security Administration assigns numbers to every American newborn child — much to the delight of illegal aliens and the document dealers who have a larger pool of numbers to falsify. The illegal aliens typically use their own names with the stolen numbers. This poses a great risk to the actual holders of the Social Security numbers and their families. It damages their credit histories and even creates tax liabilities. The IRS has been known to demand tax payments from the real owners of fraudulently used Social Security numbers (even infants and families of dead people) without regard for the fact that the identity was used illegally.

As an example, when Herman arrived in California from Mexico City with his wife and five-year-old child on a tourist visa, his intention was to live in the U.S., work, and provide a better life for his family. Without a college degree the prospects for a decent living wage in the Mexican capital are slim at best for a family of three.

He immediately connected with a document dealer in Los Angeles and was easily able to obtain phony documents, including a Social Security card and a green card. Adding insult to injury, the document dealer even told Herman the name and address of the actual owner of the Social Security number. With his American identity he landed a job with an apparel manufacturer in the Los Angeles area. He even landed a part-time job for additional money at a fast-food burger restaurant. With the unexpected high cost of living in the area,

Herman was still short of funds to provide all that his young family needed. That led him to apply for and receive government assistance to get food stamps to supplement his income. The family lived in a home overcrowded with thirteen people from four families with identical circumstances.

When Vanessa came to the United States on a tourist visa, she landed at Newark Airport from Caracas, Venezuela. She had a brother who was living in the West New York neighborhood of New Jersey, so she had a place to stay. Vanessa's intention was to escape the dire economic conditions in her home country in the pre-Hugo Chavez era, and to become a permanent resident of the United States of America. Of course, that is not what she told immigration officials. She was simply visiting a relative.

After a short while, she landed a job as a waitress in a neighborhood Latin restaurant where she could meet people while earning a salary — in cash. She was flying well below the radar. As part of her long-term plan, with her visa now expired, but with Immigration and Customs Enforcement (ICE) unable to track her down, she married an American. She remained married, but not together, long enough to obtain her green card under her real name (not Vanessa). Once she had her green card, she divorced her husband and fulfilled her "American Dream." She worked at large companies in Information Technology positions (she was a programmer in Caracas) and moved up the corporate ladder.

Daniel is a young Mexican in his twenties who came to the U.S. from Cuernavaca, Mexico, a town approximately fifty-two miles south of Mexico City. He does not speak English, but works as a busboy at an Italian restaurant in New Jersey without a problem. Once a year he returns to Cuernavaca to visit his parents and siblings. His itinerary includes traveling to Tucson and walking across the border, making sure not to be seen by border patrol agents. Once in Nogales, Mexico, the tension in his body from the risk of being nabbed by ICE disappears and he freely makes his way home. He visits Cuernavaca for two weeks and returns to his illegally adopted home in New Jersey, traveling the same route in reverse.

Daniel has been doing this for five years without getting caught. He now has several other buddies from south of the border working as busboys in the same restaurant. The others prefer not to take the risk of getting caught by traveling back and forth. They reside in the bucolic and quiet town permanently — or until they are caught and deported or until they get severely homesick and return of their own will. Homeowners in the area are pleased to subsidize their mortgages by renting a room or two to the illegal immigrants. It is a complete eco-system with a home, a job, and a nearby Western Union money transfer facility to send money home.

Regardless of their stories, the fact is that there are two sides to this coin. These young people cannot find employment in their own country, and their government does nothing to create opportunities of employment for them. Instead, the Mexican government takes comfort in seeing the U.S. do their work for them — creating an underground industry that is not so underground, and reaping an economic windfall as these illegal immigrants send billions of dollars annually back home.

The other side of the coin is the reality that the busboy jobs that Daniel, his buddies, and countless others are employed in are indeed jobs that, if they were not in the U.S. accepting a lower wage, often in cash, American youths would be filling.

The people in the government, the media, and in the general public who say that illegal immigration does not do harm to Americans and that illegal immigrants come here to work at jobs that Americans do not want to do are sugarcoating this epidemic for political expediency or, in the case of many in the general public, ignorance. In just one of the examples above, Herman perjured himself on his I-9 form, committed a felonious identity theft of someone else's Social Security number, and falsely applied for a job as an American. And this situation repeats itself in millions of cases.

In a 2002 report to Congress, the General Accounting Office stated: "INS has reported that large-scale counterfeiting has made fraudulent employment eligibility documents (e.g., Social Security cards) widely available." The Social Security Administration assumes that roughly three-quarters of illegal aliens are paying payroll taxes through withholding, which generally requires an SSN.[110]

Employers commonly turn a blind eye to the illegal use of SSNs, content to pay less wages and benefits to illegal aliens and with the confidence that they are free of culpability because the employees provided the necessary documents required in their employment applications.

However, an immigration raid at an Agriprocessors, Inc., meat processing plant in Pottsville, Iowa, in 2008 found that 76 percent of the plant's employees had bogus SSNs. And during an April 2008 raid at Pilgrim's Pride meat packing plants, more than 280 employees at facilities in five states were arrested on suspicion of committing identity theft and other criminal violations in order to obtain jobs. According to press reports, ICE agents said their investigation of Pilgrim's Pride started when the victims of identity theft came forward after having problems with taxes and credit reports.

Illegal aliens' fraudulent document use was further confirmed by Domingo Garcia, General Counsel for the League of United Latin American Citizens (LULAC), who, according to press reports, said that it was well-known that around 80 percent of the workers at Pilgrim's Pride had fake identification.[111]

The illegal immigration problem in the U.S. crosses over into the country's higher education system, as crooked documentation dealers seek to exploit the system.

On April 5, 2016, ICE arrested twenty-one people in New Jersey for allegedly conspiring with 1,000 foreigners to fraudulently maintain student visas and obtain worker visas. The federal government set up a sting operation by creating a fake university, The University of Northern New Jersey. The fake college had an impressive website and Facebook page to attract prospective students. But the college did not hold any classes and didn't have any professors.

The people arrested worked as "brokers" who solicited the university's administrators — who were actually undercover agents — to take part in the illegal scheme.

The foreigners, who it was reported by CNN were mostly from China and India, were set up by the brokers with illegal student enrollment at the fake university and fraudulent worker visas by creating employment contracts between the college and the foreign nationals.[112]

In just this one case there were 1,000 foreigners who would have skated into schools and jobs illegally, if they had not been stopped by the professional but overwhelmed agents at the Immigration and Customs Enforcement department.

There are approximately 1.2 million foreigners currently in the U.S. on legal student visas, according to the Department of Homeland Security. Unfortunately, the illegal document dealers or brokers will seek out this pool of potential customers to abuse the system by providing fraudulent work visas.

Daniel, an illegal alien from El Salvador with falsified documents enabling him to work as a mason for a hardscaping and landscaping company in the Northeast, earns $20,000 annually. That is much more than he could earn in his home country, but a fraction of what an American skilled mason commands in the Northeast region of the U.S. The salary range for a skilled mason in the Northeast region is between $51,943 and $69,920. In general, the benefit of employers hiring illegal immigrants by the millions in the United States is a benefit to the worker and to the employer, who can enjoy increased profits as a result of reduced labor costs.

It is not necessarily a benefit to the end customer, who is not paying reduced prices since the labor cost savings are not passed on to them. It also deprives the overall U.S. economy of much of those wages being recirculated into the economy. The majority of the earnings made by illegal immigrants are sent back home to the families of the workers, rather than spent in the U.S. and helping to stimulate the American economy. In fact, billions of dollars are sent to illegal workers' home countries each year. In 2008 alone, at least $2.4 billion was sent to Mexico by illegal Mexican workers.[113] And that does not consider the money that is wired to other countries including Guatemala, El Salvador, Honduras, and a host of other countries in Latin America. By 2014, the sum of money wired to Mexico by illegal immigrants skyrocketed to $26 billion.[114]

According to the Bureau of Economic Analysis, illegal immigrants residing in the U.S. send to their home countries $50 billion annually. That is a staggering amount to leave our country, bolstering the economies of the third world countries at the expense of the U.S. and Americans. Approximately a quarter of that money, or roughly $11.8 billion, is sent to El Salvador, Honduras, and Guatemala combined, adding 10 percent to each country's gross domestic product.[115]

The governments of these countries actually encourage the high levels of emigration to the U.S. because of the billions of dollars it generates for their economies! It is big business for them.

In December 2005, the Mexican government's Foreign Ministry department actually published a handbook for its citizens interested in entering the U.S. illegally. The pamphlet, *Guide for the Mexican Migrant*, advises migrants on everything from what clothes to wear if crossing the border via a river or through the desert; how to lie low once in the U.S.; how to deal with human traffickers and border patrol; and what rights they have if caught once in the U.S. They printed and distributed 1.5 million copies of the booklet throughout the country. Some in the U.S. government saw it as a move by the Mexican government to encourage the continuing export of their unemployed people and protect the inflow of billions of dollars the migrants working in the U.S. illegally send home, fueling the Mexican economy.[116]

The tragic and disingenuous misconception commonly heard is that illegal immigrants do jobs that Americans will not do. It has long been accepted that America "needs" illegal immigrants to do the work that Americans won't do. Supporters of expanded immigration and our political leaders who want to cater to the emotions of some of their constituents and even donors and the mainstream media use this argument and avoid addressing the harm that illegal immigration causes the American economy, the education system, the welfare system, and their contribution to our critical employment hardship.

In the examples I stated above about Daniel, Herman, and Vanessa, are they doing jobs that Americans will not do, or are they doing jobs that Americans will not do at the depressed wages that employers are paying the illegal immigrants? By leaving wages out of the picture, the supporters of immigration and the political leaders who for decades have failed to address the issue cling to an argument that applies to the days when temporary migrant workers picked the crops that farmers grew. That argument, though those making the case have conveniently extended it to all industries infiltrated by illegal immigrants, does not apply to landscapers; or fast-food employees; or restaurant waiters and busboys; or construction workers. These are jobs that Americans will gladly do, so long as the employers are willing to pay wages that are commensurate with those positions in the U.S. economy.

President Barack Obama and Hillary Clinton, when she was Secretary of State or senator from New York, have done little to address the damaging issue of illegal immigration. Neither have any of their predecessors, regardless of party affiliation.

Hillary Clinton, in her campaign for the 2016 presidency of the United States, has made an issue of Republican candidate Donald Trump's pledge to build a wall along the U.S. southern border with Mexico and deport the millions of illegal immigrants residing in the U.S. Clinton proclaimed, with a tone of disbelief and disgust, "I will stand up against any effort to deport dreamers. Immigrants are vital to our economy." It is a position that on the surface sounds humane, until sensible Americans consider the complete impact of her words. Americans cannot afford to allow Clinton to pull on their heartstrings by purposely and deceptively confusing Immigration with Illegal Immigration. They are two vastly different concepts.

Does Clinton truly believe that illegal immigration is "vital to our economy," or is she purposely blending illegal immigration into America's fabric of legal immigration that made this country great? Clearly, she chooses to ignore the devastating impact, only some of which has been written about in this book, in an effort to win the votes of the liberal people, especially Hispanics, who perhaps are not considering the true cost of illegal immigration.

By calling the illegal immigrants dreamers, Hillary Clinton insults the millions of legal immigrants who came to the United States to build new lives and make this country home.

The hard fact is that no president will be able to fix the problem faced by millions of unemployed Americans without rectifying the epidemic that is illegal immigration. Americans would certainly understand the issue, and accept the remedy required to reverse it, if politicians would be willing to communicate it clearly, and lay out a plan to fix it. A plan to provide a path to citizenship, as Hillary Clinton advocates, will not fix the constant and growing flow into the United States of illegal immigrants.

Hillary Clinton is misleading the American people when she campaigns and promises to create jobs for unemployed people, but simultaneously pledges to create a path to citizenship for illegal immigrants.

These two issues, or challenges facing Americans, are not mutually exclusive.

The recommendations that Clinton proposes, while making good sound bites to her supporters, do not get to the root of the problem. They validate her experience as a politician and not as a problem-solver.

To be realistic, the issue of illegal immigration cannot be addressed simply on our side of the border. People who are desperate economically in their own countries will find a way to migrate elsewhere in search of a more prosperous life. That is simply survival. Our leaders must work with leaders of other countries like Mexico, Guatemala, Honduras, El Salvador, and other Central American nations to assist them in addressing the level of poverty and lack of economic opportunity of their own people.

During his campaign for the presidency of Mexico, the current President Enrique Pena-Nieto pledged to lift 15 million Mexicans out of poverty. From 2012 to 2014, the first two years of his six-year term (a Mexican president cannot seek a second term), the poverty level grew by 0.7 percentage point to 46.2 from 45.5 percent in 2012. With a population of nearly 120 million people, that equates to 55.3 million people in the country who live in poverty. Poverty in Mexico is defined as living on no more than 2,542 pesos a month, which is approximately $157.70 in cities such as Mexico City, and 1,615 pesos in rural areas. People who live in extreme poverty live on 1,243 pesos a month in cities and 868 pesos ($53) in rural areas. While 46.2 percent is the national average for poverty levels, there are regions like Chiapas and Oaxaca that have poverty levels of 76.2 and 66.8, respectively. That is of a population of 3.4 million people in Chiapas and 3.8 million in Oaxaca. These people, with no clear path to a better life, will risk their lives to get to the U.S.[117]

The poverty level in Guatemala, a country that borders Mexico to the south, and whose citizens enter the U.S. illegally through the Mexico-U.S. border, is 54 percent of a total population of 15.47 million people. El Salvador's poverty level is 31 percent of a total population of 6.34 million people.

America needs political leaders who are willing to pressure these countries to not only control their own borders, but also devote resources to create opportunities to lift their people out of poverty. And since the gateway to America's illegal immigration epidemic is Mexico, we need leaders to work with the Mexican government on realistic and constructive programs to create an environment where the Mexican people at the lower rungs of the economic ladder have a path to a better life. The reality today is that the people living in poverty in Mexico represent a drain on the economy. The Mexican government, at least by not following through on its customary, but empty, promises to reduce poverty, encourages and likely prefers that this economic drain be diverted north of the border.

By promising to build a wall that he says he will have Mexico pay for, and to deport all illegal immigrants currently residing in the United States, Donald J. Trump has hit a nerve with the American people as the leading candidate for the Republican nomination for President of the United States. When Trump first made that campaign pledge, most people responded with astonishment because it sounded contrary to the political correctness they were accustomed to hearing from politicians. Some in the media and in Washington laughed at Trump as an outsider, inexperienced at politics and prone to this type of "insensitive" rhetoric. They expected his candidacy to gradually (hopefully quickly) fade away.

What Trump's detractors did not see coming is that millions of Americans, after giving thought to his position on illegal immigration, international trade, and jobs, began to identify and agree with his message. Americans finally heard from a presidential candidate what they had been thinking: that illegal immigration is a drain on the American economy; it has caused unnecessary crime in our cities; and it has taken jobs away from Americans. Whether Trump will win the Republican nomination for president and then win the election to become the next President of the United States, and make good on his pledge to build a wall along the border that Mexico will pay for and deport 11 million illegal immigrants (actually, it's more like 20 million) remains to be seen. But, there is no question that Trump has raised the awareness of the American people on this problem facing the country.

He has awakened the people and stoked their anger against the establishment in Washington, who has let them down for far too long. Trump has given many Americans hope that a tough, problem-solving businessman, with all his business acumen, negotiating talents, and knack for recognizing problems at their root, is just what the country needs.

Part of the anger that the American people burn with comes from the realization that despite the Washington rhetoric, little has been done to improve the economic conditions of so many who have been forgotten or ignored in the aftermath of the Great Recession of 2008. How could the greatest country in the world itself have a poverty rate of 14.8 percent as of 2014, according to the U.S. Census Bureau? Of a population of approximately 320 million, 46.7 million Americans live in poverty. Paradoxically, that is approximately 9 million less than the number of people impoverished in Mexico.[118]

What Americans sorely need from the next president is the business acumen and creativity to work with the private sector to create jobs that will once and for all put an end to the desperate hardship of the long-term unemployed and grossly underemployed. One area that is primed for negotiation in this regard is the $2.1 trillion in profits that the 500 largest American companies have parked overseas to avoid paying U.S. taxes.

These firms have generated those profits overseas, where they have already paid taxes on that income. They do not want to pay taxes twice and at a much higher U.S. rate.

There is leverage on both sides that the president and Congress have not made an effort to take advantage of on behalf of the American people. The companies don't want to pay taxes if they repatriate those overseas funds, and America needs jobs. Perhaps the next president will, as part of the administration's multi-pronged strategy to restore the American dream for all, negotiate with the companies on a mutually beneficial solution. The reality is that the jobs crisis has been created and compounded by a series of factors, and many of these can be reversed with effort and collaboration between the federal government and large corporations in the private sector.

These are corporations who hire, either directly or as subcontractors, many of the roughly 650,000 H-1B work visa holders, outsource a significant amount of technology and other back office functions to overseas firms, and continually reduce their American workforce as they outsource more and more functions to other countries — all in the interest of increasing profits by reducing labor costs.

Here is another example of why Donald Trump has become so popular with angry Americans on the 2016 presidential campaign trail:

Since 2000, the U.S. has lost approximately 5 million manufacturing jobs. That is on top of the many millions lost to countries like China and Mexico in prior years. In effect, the American dream has been exported. General Electric pays a 24-year-old college-educated engineer at a GE plant in Mexico the equivalent of $1,500 a month or $18,000 annually. That same job in the U.S. costs GE $75,000 annually, about four times what GE pays that engineer in Mexico, where GE employs 10,000 Mexicans across seventeen manufacturing plants. Trump has promised to bring those types of jobs back to America.[119]

The companies with the largest funds in overseas profits include Apple, GE, Microsoft, Pfizer, and three-quarters of the American corporations on the Fortune 500 list. Collectively, these companies stand to pay an estimated $620 billion in U.S. taxes if they repatriate the funds.[120]

The next president can summon the CEOs of these companies to the White House and strike a deal on behalf of the American people. He can offer them a moratorium on U.S. taxes on repatriated funds for a period of time, perhaps two years. In exchange, the corporations — all of them — would use the tax savings, and then some, to employ Americans, not for incremental jobs necessarily, but to reduce the amount of outsourcing and the use of H-1B resources. Those jobs which have been effectively taken away from Americans would be returned to them. That will encourage the American firms to invest in jobs here at home, circulate the wages into the U.S. economy, boost the morale of American workers and their families, and reduce the level of unemployment and underemployment. Part of that effort, which I will call the Patriotic Repatriation of Trillions, should also include an agreement to keep these large corporations from relocating plants and headquarters to other lower-wage and lower-tax countries, when it is done simply to reduce labor costs.

Too often these decisions to relocate jobs and displace American workers are made without consideration of the many benefits in tax concessions and subsidies that the U.S. government provides to corporations here. That should not be ignored.

For example, President Obama's Department of Energy awarded Carrier Corporation — manufacturer of heating and air-conditioning products and a unit of United Technologies Corp. — in 2013 $5.1 million in clean energy tax credits for its Indianapolis facility. Carrier's plan was to use the money to "expand production at its Indianapolis plant to meet increasing demand for its eco-friendly condensing gas furnace product line." One can only imagine that the 1,400 employees at the Indianapolis facility were excited by the injection of government funds that would logically result in more work for them.[121]

Yet, in February of 2016, Carrier announced that it was shifting the 1,400 jobs from the Indianapolis plant and 700 from a plant in Huntington, Indiana, to Monterrey,

Mexico. According to union leaders for the American workers, Carrier expects to pay the Mexican workers the equivalent of $3 per hour compared to an average of over $20 per hour for the U.S. workers.

Carrier is only one of many U.S. manufacturers moving jobs to Mexico. However, videos of a company official delivering the news to the Indianapolis plant's stunned workforce, posted on YouTube, provided a vivid look at the pain and anger such decisions cause.[122]

The same month that Carrier announced its decision to shift U.S. jobs to Mexico, auto giant Ford announced that it would be building a new assembly plant in San Luis Potosi, Mexico, and expanding an existing facility near Mexico City. According to *The Wall Street Journal*, Ford will double the number of autos produced in Mexico by adding half a million units of annual capacity by the year 2018. The move of both companies, Ford and Carrier, has come in the midst of the 2016 presidential campaign season and has heightened the debate over cheaper foreign labor. As with the employment of illegal immigrants and many H-1B visa holders in the U.S., the attraction of cheaper labor on either side of our border is motivated by a desire to increase profits and satisfy shareholders, at the expense of American workers and consumers, who have lost jobs and are not paying less for the products.

The result of the economic devastation that many Americans are experiencing is anger at the Washington politicians, who are seen as not representing the people adequately enough to address the issues, compounded by a lack of confidence that our leaders will keep America safe from radical Islamic terrorism. It has created a perfect storm for a revolt against the establishment, giving rise and unexpected support to outsider candidates like Donald Trump and Ted Cruz on the Republican side, and Bernie Sanders on the Democratic side.

The American people feel compelled to try a different approach to resolving the country's problems, and these three candidates are seen as providing the best chance at that. Even though Hillary Clinton is leading in the delegate count against Sanders in the Democratic primaries, she is viewed by the majority of Americans as untrustworthy and an unfavorable candidate. Her unfavorable rating is running at 55 percent, according to polls compiled by a Huffpost pollster. Donald Trump, the leading candidate on the Republican side based on the number of delegates he has accumulated in the primaries, also has a high unfavorable rating. He clocks in with a rating of 58 percent unfavorable, according to Huffpost.

The difference between the two leading candidates is that Trump is offering the American people a businessman's response and a CEO approach to leading the country. His campaign slogan "Make America Great Again" has resonated with voters in the primaries because it gives them hope that a President Trump will restore prosperity to the economy, producing jobs and creating opportunities for Americans to thrive once again. Trump has pledged to create a wall on the U.S.-Mexican border to keep illegal aliens from entering the country, and to deport the illegals who are residing in the U.S. Whether this is feasible or not doesn't matter at the moment. The sheer possibility that all those jobs that are stolen from Americans by illegal immigrants will be returned after Trump deports the millions of illegals who now have them is resonating with many people.

Trump has created a nationalistic fervor that has spawned a revolution among the people who are hungry to take back the country — from illegals, non-Americans such as H-1B visa holders who are draining higher-level jobs, companies that are sending jobs overseas to outsourcing giants in countries like India, and from politicians who owe favors to big corporate donors and lobbyists.

Trump's unfavorable rating is derived from his bluntness, which makes him come across as politically incorrect. The millions of Americans who support him do not seem to care enough about that, especially if he will do what he is pledging to do: Make America Great Again. Numerous people who have voted Democratic in past presidential elections have told me they will vote for Trump this year if he becomes the Republican nominee, as he has a good chance of becoming.

Riding the wave of massive discontent among Americans is Senator Bernie Sanders on the Democratic side. Although he has been a member of Congress for nearly twenty-four years (sixteen in the House of Representatives and nearly eight in the Senate), he was relatively unknown when he declared his candidacy for president in the 2016 campaign. He is a lifelong Independ-Independent, but decided to run as a Democrat to oppose Hillary Clinton. He considers himself a Democratic socialist, and his views against the establishment in Washington, big corporations, and Wall Street have taken root throughout the campaign in a political year in which Americans prefer to send an outsider to the White House.

The American people are fed up with politicians who make campaign promises and then do not keep them. Instead they play politics and make speeches and give press conferences to attempt to convince Americans that they are doing everything possible to help the people.

The next president will face significant but surmountable challenges. The American people are craving a leader who truly cares about the country — enough to work with Congress to deliver real solutions that will make the country better for all Americans. That must include reducing the national debt; resolving or at least improving the illegal immigration condition; improving business opportunities for corporations to keep their operations here and repatriate the trillions of earnings held overseas; restoring relationships with America's foreign allies; and protecting Americans from terrorism both here and abroad by acknowledging the threat of radical Islamic terrorism and confronting that challenge to defeat the terrorists. That should include a serious campaign with Muslim nations friendly with the U.S. to get them on the front lines of the war against Al Qaeda and ISIS and conquer that enemy.

Our next president must be committed to restoring America's greatness. He must be entirely focused on these issues and more.

All Americans are depending on that, which is why Donald Trump, with his Make America Great Again slogan, has excited so many voters.

Epilogue

The American people are by and large an optimistic people. Despite the many challenges that the country faces — the decimation of the middle class; the erosion of the American dream; the constant fight against terrorism; and the stagnation in the political system — Americans continue to believe that with the right leadership, these challenges can be overcome. The American people continue to have faith that the future will be brighter with the right leader in the White House.

By late March 2016, the list of candidates for the nomination for President of the United States was down to three on the Republican side and two on the Democratic side. Still running among the Republicans are the frontrunner Donald Trump, the second-place candidate Ted Cruz, and John Kasich, governor of Ohio, who is the only one among the three to be considered, based on his long career in government service, as the establishment candidate.

On the Democratic side, the primary race between the leading, but highly unfavorably rated, establishment candidate Hillary Clinton and popular Democratic socialist Bernie Sanders is tightening. Clinton is a damaged candidate, with the FBI investigation of her email server scandal anticipated to reach a conclusion in the coming weeks.

With Trump being the ultimate outsider, popular with his millions of supporters but unpopular and unwanted by the party leaders, it is still possible that both parties will end up with contested conventions.

A contested convention will keep the door open for each party to put up for nomination a savior to represent each side for the push to the November election. Each party has its own objective.

Barack Obama, as the leader of the Democratic Party, is eager to see a candidate who can be the next president in his own image. He is looking for someone who can continue his policies for the country. With his deep dislike and mistrust of Hillary and Bill Clinton, there is good reason why he has not endorsed Hillary's candidacy. He knows full well that given the animosity between the two families, including Michelle Obama's hatred of the Clintons, a Clinton presidency will veer away from Obama's policies, if only for the sake of vengeance.

In his book *Blood Feud*, journalist Edwin Klein writes about the dysfunctional, jealous relationship between the Clintons and Obamas and the suspicion that could culminate in dramatically altering the face of the 2016 presidential race.

Klein writes that "outwardly, they put on a show of unity — but privately, the Obamas and Clintons, the two power couples of the Democratic Party, loathe each other."

"I hate that man Obama more than any man I've ever met, more than any man who ever lived," Bill Clinton said to friends on one occasion, adding he would never forgive Obama for suggesting he was a racist during the 2008 campaign.

"The feeling is mutual. Obama made excuses not to talk to Bill, while the first lady privately sniped about Hillary," writes Klein.

"On most evenings, Michelle Obama and her trusted adviser, Valerie Jarrett, met in a quiet corner of the White House residence. They'd usually open a bottle of Chardonnay, catch up on news about Sasha and Malia, and gossip about people who gave them heartburn."

Their favorite bête noire was Hillary Clinton, whom they nicknamed "Hildebeest," after the menacing and shaggy-maned gnu that roams the Serengeti.

Bill Clinton complained about being ignored by President Obama.

"I've had two successors since I left the White House — Bush and Obama — and I've heard more from Bush, asking for my advice, than I've heard from Obama. I have no relationship with the president — none whatsoever," Clinton said.

On one rare occasion when Obama begrudgingly invited Bill Clinton to a round of golf during his 2012 re-election campaign, Bill took the opportunity to press Obama to help him and Hillary for their anticipated 2016 run for the White House.

"Bill got into it right away," said a Clinton family friend. "He told Obama, 'Hillary and I are gearing up for a run in 2016.' He said Hillary would be 'the most qualified, most experienced candidate, perhaps in history.' His reference to Hillary's experience made Obama wince, since it was clearly a shot at his lack of experience when he ran for president.

"And so Bill continued to talk about Hillary's qualifications and the coming campaign in 2016. But Barack didn't bite. He changed the subject several times. Then suddenly, Barack said something that took Bill by complete surprise. He said, 'You know, Michelle would make a great presidential candidate, too.'

"Bill was speechless. Was Barack comparing Michelle's qualifications to Hillary's? Bill said that if he hadn't been on a mission to strike a deal with Barack, he might have stormed off the golf course then and there."

Bill Clinton had become convinced that Obama wouldn't endorse Hillary in 2016. During a gathering at Whitehaven (the Clintons' home in D.C.), guests overheard Bill talking to his daughter, Chelsea, about whether the president would back Joe Biden.

"Recently, I've been hearing a different scenario from state committeemen," Clinton said. "They say he's looking for a candidate who's just like him. Someone relatively unknown. Someone with a fresh face.

"He's convinced himself he's been a brilliant president, and wants to clone himself — to find his Mini-Me."

Bill told Chelsea, "He's hunting for someone to succeed him, and he believes the American people don't want to vote for someone who's been around for a long time. He thinks that your mother and I are what he calls 'so 20th century.' He's looking for another Barack Obama."[123]

Fast-forward from then to the present and there is no surprise as to why Hillary has yet to receive an endorsement or any support from Obama. If she falters, either due to the FBI investigation over her use of a private email server or because Bernie Sanders prevents her from avoiding a contested convention, we can expect Joe Biden to rise to the occasion at the convention.

On the other side, the Republicans are planning for a contested convention as a means of presenting their own White Knight in Cleveland, Ohio. They do not want either of the top two candidates, Trump and Cruz, to win the nomination and represent the party in the general election.

They may be underestimating Trump, or he may be underestimating the power games of the party. Bits of information have been leaking out that the party prefers that House Speaker Paul Ryan be their nominee.

The people shall see! Ryan has repeatedly stated that he does not want the nomination. That is the same position he held before accepting to be Speaker — for the good of the party.

In the end, Donald J. Trump will prevail and make the Republican party his party.

The Democratic and Republican parties must not underestimate the will of the American people. The challenges facing the country are about the people and not about the political parties. America needs a great leader who will be able to unite us all in meeting the difficult challenges ahead. America needs a leader who sincerely and passionately believes that the government's principle function is to serve The People.

It was the great Ronald Reagan who acknowledged: "Government's first duty is to protect the people, not run their lives."[124]

ACKNOWLEDGEMENTS

First and foremost, I want to thank my wife, Estela, for her dedicated support and encouragement during the writing of this book. Her patience and commentary throughout multiple readings of the manuscript were most valuable.

I would also like to thank Reba Hilbert for her help and dedication in editing and tweaking the manuscript, and to Stephane Coic for his commitment to work on the cover and for his friendship.

In writing this book I consulted a number of books and many articles and websites that provided valuable information and observations. While all are captured in the Notes section of the book, I want to especially acknowledge the following books: *Exceptional: Why the World Needs a Powerful America*, by Dick Cheney and Liz Cheney; *The Audacity of Hope: Thoughts on Reclaiming the American Dream* by Barack Obama; *Dreams From My Father, A Story of Race and Inheritance* by Barack Obama; and *The Roots of Obama's Rage* by Dinesh D'Souza. Some of the events that found their way into the book were captured in real time as I watched CNN, CNBC, or Fox News. Online platforms such as YouTube provided another means of researching past events.

All of the research that has gone into the production of this book serves to remind all Americans that we must seek leaders who will manage the country's business on behalf of the people. And that careful consideration should be given to address challenges at their root and not just treat symptoms.

About the Author

Israel Vicente is a technology entrepreneur and founder of GCS, a successful global IT consulting firm based in New Jersey. He is an avid reader, world traveler, and researcher. In his role as CEO of GCS, Israel has had the opportunity to speak to many people of all income levels throughout the U.S. and abroad, giving him a firsthand perspective of their experiences, successes, and hardships.

In 2013, he decided to dedicate any spare time he could find to becoming a published author. On long-distance flights to visit with customers, he replaced the previously customary glass or two of wine with a pen and a notebook. In 2014, he published two well-received nonfiction books, The Courage to Be Different and Divergent Lives.

Israel has always been interested in politics and how it impacts the lives of people everywhere. The lead-up to the 2016 presidential contest served as inspiration for his third book, For the People - Time to Take Our Country Back! He lives in New Jersey with his wife and children.

Endnotes

1 https://en.wikipedia.org/wiki/Gettysburg_Address

2 As reported by CBS News, read the article at www.cbsnews.com/news/national-debt-up-6-trillion-since-obama-took-office/

3 *The Washington Post*, article by Charles Ornstein and Hagit Limor March 31, 2011

4 From "Obama Administration Hits Another Grim Record on Lack of Government Transparency," a column in Townhall.com on March 18, 2015. Full story available at http://townhall.com/tipsheet/katiepavlich/2015/03/18/united-states-hits-another-grim-record-on-lack-of-government-transparency-n1972697

5 Published in *The Hill*, February 14, 2013, Obama says his is 'most transparent administration' ever. Full article available at http://thehill.com/blogs/blog-briefing-room/news/283335-obama-this-is-the-most-transparent-administration-in-history

6 *Politfact* Florida article on September 24, 2012. Full article available on www.politifact.com/florida/statements/2012/sep/24/barack-obama/barack-obama-said-fast-and-furious-began-under-bus/

7 www.newsmax.com/FastFeatures/barack-obama-scandal-atf-fast-and-furious/2014/12/28/id/613434/

8 https://en.wikipedia.org/wiki/ATF_gunwalking_scandal

9 Ibid.

10 www.cbsnews.com/news/fast-and-furious-gun-found-at-mexican-crime-scene/

11 www.foxnews.com/politics/2016/01/20/rifle-capable-taking-down-helicopter-found-at-el-chapo-hideout-purchased-through-fast-and-furious-program.html

12 www.newsmax.com/FastFeatures/barack-obama-scandal-atf-fast-and-furious/2014/12/28/id/613434/

13 *The Roots of Obama's Rage* by Dinesh D'Souza, pg. 44

14 www.factcheck.org/2013/11/keeping-your-health-plan/

[15] www.usnews.com/debate-club/is-obamacare-working

[16] Obama keep his health plan:
www.politifact.com/wisconsin/statements/2013/oct/21/sean-duffy/obamacare-congress-must-buy-insurance-marketplaces/

[17] http://abcnews.go.com/Politics/president-obama-vows-completely-decapitate-isis-operations/story?id=35173579

[18] *Exceptional, Why the World Needs a Powerful America* by Dick Cheney and Liz Cheney, pg. 169

[19] www.usatoday.com/story/news/2015/11/16/obama-g-20-news-conference-turkey-paris-attacks-terrorism/75863678/

[20] Read entire article with full context and sources at www.politifact.com/truth-o-meter/statements/2014/sep/07/barack-obama/what-obama-said-about-islamic-state-jv-team/

[21] www.usatoday.com/story/news/2015/11/16/obama-g-20-news-conference-turkey-paris-attacks-terrorism/75863678/

[22] www.ijreview.com/2015/02/251741-isis-terrorists/

[23] https://en.wikipedia.org/wiki/ISIL_beheading_incidents

[24] *Exceptional*, pg. 138

[25] *Exceptional*, pg. 140

[26] *Exceptional*, pg. 141

[27] Ibid.

[28] *Exceptional*, pg. 145

[29] www.washingtontimes.com/news/2014/sep/10/america-feel-more-unsafe-anytime-911-ready-militar/

[30] www.newsweek.com/panettas-memoir-blasts-obama-his-leadership-blames-him-state-iraq-and-syria-276582

[31] http://nation.foxnews.com/2015/11/23/fmr-dia-director-who-briefed-president-rise-isis-has-harsh-words-obama

[32] www.washingtonpost.com/politics/an-angry-obama-upbraids-critics-who-want-to-block-refugees-from-syria/2015/11/18/c2375082-8db9-11e5-acff-673ae92ddd2b_story.html

[33] *The Audacity of Hope: Thoughts on Reclaiming the American Dream* by Barack Obama, front inside flap

[34] *Exceptional*, pgs. 162-163

[35] *Exceptional*, pg. 163

36 *Exceptional*, pg. 163

37 *Exceptional*, pg. 165

38 From *Dreams From My Father: A Story of Race and Inheritance* by Barack Obama, pgs. 40-41

39 www.washingtonpost.com/politics/an-angry-obama-upbraids-critics-who-want-to-block-refugees-from-syria/2015/11/18/c2375082-8db9-11e5-acff-673ae92ddd2b_story.html

40 www.huffingtonpost.com/entry/dianne-feinstein-isis-stronger_56521fe6e4b0879a5b0b6492

41 www.cnn.com/2015/11/19/politics/house-democrats-refugee-hearings-obama/

42 http://abcnews.go.com/Politics/terrorism-fears-rise-post-paris-back-force-oppose/story?id=35327667

43 http://money.cnn.com/2015/12/18/media/president-obama-off-record-meeting/index.html

44 www.cnn.com/2016/01/07/us/terror-charges-refugees/

45 http://thehill.com/blogs/blog-briefing-room/news/251634-obamas-approval-rating-falls-in-new-poll

46 *Exceptional*, pg. 150

47 www.thedailybeast.com/articles/2015/09/09/exclusive-50-spies-say-isis-intelligence-was-cooked.html

48 http://thehill.com/policy/defense/253188-report-analysts-claim-us-military-altering-intelligence-on-isis-war

49 http://dailycaller.com/2015/10/23/benghazi-victims-family-members-blast-clinton-after-hearing-video/

50 Excerpted from the article by Factcheck.org. The full article and its sources can be accessed on www.factcheck.org/2012/10/benghazi-timeline/

51 *Exceptional*, pg. 157

52 *The Audacity of Hope*, pg. 279

53 *Exceptional*, pg. 125

54 www.latimes.com/nation/politics/politicsnow/la-na-obamachildhood15-2007mar15-story.html

55 www.danielpipes.org/11952/obama-muslim-childhood

56 *Dreams From My Father*, pgs. 406-407

[57] *Exceptional*, pg. 127

[58] www.amnestyusa.org/our-work/countries/americas/nicaragua

[59] *Exceptional*, pg. 127

[60] www.politico.com/magazine/story/2015/01/where-was-obama-when-the-middle-class-needed-him-114502

[61] http://money.cnn.com/infographic/economy/what-is-middle-class-anyway/

[62] http://money.cnn.com/infographic/economy/what-is-middle-class-anyway/

[63] www.gallup.com/opinion/chairman/181469/big-lie-unemployment.aspx

[64] www.nytimes.com/2015/01/26/business/economy/middle-class-shrinks-further-as-more-fall-out-instead-of-climbing-up.html?_r=0

[65] www.nytimes.com/2015/01/26/business/economy/middle-class-shrinks-further-as-more-fall-out-instead-of-climbing-up.html?_r=0

[66] www.cnbc.com/2015/10/02/

[67] www.usnews.com/news/the-report/articles/2015/07/16/unemployment-is-low-but-more-workers-are-leaving-the-workforce

[68] www.washingtontimes.com/news/2015/jan/4/obama-economy-welfare-dependency-peaks-as-rich-get/?page=all

[69] *The Roots of Obama's Rage*, pg. 175

[70] www.ijreview.com/2014/05/138996-obama-1er-438-increase-wealth-since-taking-office/

[71] www.washingtonpost.com/news/the-fix/wp/2014/06/05/is-the-american-dream-dead/

[72] *The Roots of Obama's Rage*, pg. 186

[73] http://data.worldbank.org/indicator/SH.XPD.TOTL.ZS

[74] https://en.wikipedia.org/wiki/Barack_Obama,_Sr.

[75] *The Roots of Obama's Rage*, pg. 63

[76] *Dreams From My Father*, pg. 220

[77] Ibid., pg. 278

[78] Ibid., pg. 230

[79] Ibid., pg. 220

[80] www.wvwnews.net/story.php?id=5991

[81] *Dreams From My Father*, pgs. 214-215

[82] www.factcheck.org/2015/02/obama-and-american-exceptionalism/

[83] www.newsweek.com/kenyan-leaders-respond-obamas-support-lgbt-rights-357563

[84] www.youtube.com/watch?v=4rrvQTsiGCs

[85] Ibid., pg. 418

[86] www.dailymail.co.uk/news/article-1091499/Barack-Obamas-grandfather-tortured-British-Kenyas-Mau-Mau-rebellion.html

[87] Ibid., pg. 406

[88] www.telegraph.co.uk/news/worldnews/barackobama/4623148/Barack-Obama-sends-bust-of-Winston-Churchill-on-its-way-back-to-Britain.html

[89] https://en.wikipedia.org/wiki/Family_of_Barack_Obama

[90] www.npr.org/2011/07/11/137553552/president-obamas-father-a-bold-and-reckless-life

See also *The Other Barack: The Bold and Reckless Life of President Obama's Father*, by Sally H. Jacobs

[91] www.washingtontimes.com/news/2012/sep/11/obama-my-muslim-faith/?page=all

[92] *Exceptional*, pg. 125

[93] www.space.com/8725-nasa-chief-bolden-muslim-remark-al-jazeera-stir.html

[94] Ibid.

[95] www.usnews.com/news/articles/2015/07/14/iran-nuclear-deal-makes-middle-east-allies-nervous

[96] www.cnn.com/2007/POLITICS/01/31/biden.obama/

[97] *Obama's America* by Dinesh D'Souza, pgs. 136-137 with pictures in between

[98] https://en.wikipedia.org/wiki/Frank_Marshall_Davis

[99] http://thecaucus.blogs.nytimes.com/2008/03/24/clinton-misspoke-about-bosnia-trip-campaign-says/?_r=0

[100] www.newsweek.com/barack-obama-how-he-did-it-85083

[101] www.newyorker.com/magazine/2012/09/10/lets-be-friends

[102] www.newsweek.com/barack-obama-how-he-did-it-85083

[103] *Exceptional*, pgs. 156-160

[104] https://en.wikipedia.org/wiki/Hillary_Clinton_email_controversy

[105] Ibid.

[106] www.cbsnews.com/news/campaign-2016-hillary-clinton-ive-always-tried-to-tell-the-truth/

[107] www.cbsnews.com/news/obama-mocks-gop-jokes-they-want-border-moat/

[108] www.washingtonpost.com/blogs/plum-line/wp/2015/10/20/what-hillarys-claim-that-republicans-are-her-enemies-is-really-about/

[109] www.cairco.org/issues/how-many-illegal-aliens-reside-united-states

[110] http://cis.org/IdentityTheft

[111] Ibid.

[112] http://money.cnn.com/2016/04/05/pf/college/visa-scam-fake-university/index.html?iid=hp-stack-dom

[113] http://cis.org/IdentityTheft

[114] www.cairco.org/issues/remittances

[115] http://immigrationreform.com/2014/10/29/illegal-immigrants-send-home-50-billion-annually-but-cost-taxpayers-more-than-113-billion/

[116] Ibid.

[117] www.reuters.com/article/us-mexico-poverty-idUSKCN0PX2B320150723

[118] www.census.gov/hhes/www/poverty/about/overview/

[119] http://money.cnn.com/2016/03/31/news/economy/mexico-us-globalization-wage-gap/

[120] www.reuters.com/article/us-usa-tax-offshore-idUSKCN0S008U20151006

[121] www.breitbart.com/big-government/2016/02/15/carrier-received-5-1-million-in-obama-stimulus-cash/

[122] http://nypost.com/2016/02/16/huge-pay-cut-fuels-carriers-move-to-mexico/

[123] http://nypost.com/2014/06/21/inside-the-jealous-feud-between-the-obamas-and-hildebeest-clintons/

[124] "Ronald Reagan." BrainyQuote.com. Xplore Inc., 2016. 20 April 2016. www.brainyquote.com/quotes/authors/r/ronald_reagan.html

Made in the USA
Charleston, SC
20 June 2016